Dear Rabbi and Susan...

101 Real-Life
Ask the Rabbi Questions

by
Rabbi Daniel Lapin
Susan Lapin

Lifecodex Publishing, LLC

Table of Contents

Table of Contents Continued...

Questions & Answers About Faith

Table of Contents Continued...

Questions & Answers About Friends

Table of Contents Continued...

Acknowledgements

While the idea of pulling together this book has percolated for a long time, our talented friend, Christian Ophus, stepped in and turned it into a reality. In addition to designing a cover that we love, he chose and collated the questions and answers in this volume. Thank you, Christian.

Our amazing assistant, Crystol Harrison, has made our lives both easier and more pleasant over the past few years. More recently, Rose Angove has joined our team allowing us to spend even more time on writing and teaching. We are more grateful for the help provided us by these two remarkable people than they can possibly know.

Most of all, we thank HaShem (God) for His many blessings. We are daily grateful for His behind the scenes machinations that let a girl from New York and a boy from South Africa meet in California. Among our greatest blessing are our wonderful children, sons-in-law and grandchildren. Each and every one of them lights up our lives each and every day. That they are close to one another while following in our spiritual footsteps is a tribute to their steadfast loyalty and a source of deep happiness for us.

We would be remiss if we did not also thank those of you who trusted us with your questions and who constantly strive to follow God's guidance in all the different parts of your life.

We love hearing responses to Thought Tools, Susan's Musings and our books, audio and DVD resources. Your comments and affectionate support give us much strength.

Introduction

While visiting Israel, we were enjoying a meal with friends when our hosts pulled out a wooden box and six accompanying wooden shapes. One by one, everyone at the table tried, unsuccessfully, to fit the pieces into the box. Although we knew that there was a solution, we simply couldn't find it. Finally, one of the teenagers at the table persisted and solved the puzzle. Once we saw the answer, it seemed obvious.

Life throws puzzles at us constantly. Unlike the brainteaser above, the consequences of being stumped can be enormous. Sometimes not being able to see a solution means that we are estranged from family or friends, or we do less well financially than we should. Other times, our confusion interferes with our relationship with God or leads us down the wrong path.

Over the years, we have received thousands of letters asking for our guidance. Usually, the questions stem from a desire to be better—a better human being, spouse, parent, employee, money-earner or friend. The questions range from the curious to major life dilemmas. With time and space limitations and no opportunity for clarification, we aren't able to provide unequivocal answers. Rather, we try to supply perspective, add useful insights and suggest avenues to explore.

Our 'Ask the Rabbi' column has been so popular that we have decided to compile 101 of the questions and answers into this book. In some cases, we have slightly updated questions and our responses, while in others we have taken advantage of the opportunity to expand on our original answer. We hope this book serves to provoke conversation and thought and as a reminder that facing and overcoming challenges is a shared human endeavor.

Thanks for trusting us with your questions,

Rabbi Daniel and Susan Lapin

Questions & Answers
About Family

1.
I Want Guests, My Wife Doesn't

I live in the Bay area, which is a popular tourist destination. I would welcome having visitors as guests in our home but my wife absolutely rejects the idea. She gets all stressed about it.

Isn't it a good or Godly deed to host old friends or relatives? What are your thoughts on this?

M.

Dear M,

Oh, we have so many thoughts on this. While we love hearing from you, we really think that you should be speaking to your wife and not to us.

You are certainly correct that God looks kindly on hospitality and kindness to others. There are also many other deeds that make Him smile. Just to give you a few ideas, do you regularly visit the sick and religiously give charity? Are you a Big Brother and do you offer handyman help to any neighbors who might be widowed? The point we are making is that there are many ways in which to reach out to others and we all tend towards ones that fit our time, talents and personalities. You might enjoy having guests, but perhaps your wife would prefer cooking for new mothers or driving an elderly neighbor to a doctor's appointment as her "Godly deed" activity.

We personally love having guests. Even so, as Susan began devoting more hours to creating and editing our teaching resources, we have not extended ourselves in this area as much as we used to. None of us can do everything. You may be picturing sitting and chatting with relatives and your wife may be picturing extra laundry, cooking and clean-up. Or perhaps she relishes quiet time at home because her days are hectic. We don't know why she doesn't want guests, but we suggest you find out without being critical and implying a lack in her for not wanting them. If it is a matter as simple as doing laundry, you can assure her that you will take care of it. If it doesn't fit her personality or her current schedule, then the two of you might decide that she will welcome your childhood best friend and you won't even ask about having over that second cousin with whom you never speak.

This difference of opinion is an opportunity for the two of you to learn more about each other and to show how much you value each other's desires. The discussion can be glue that holds you together rather than a wedge that drives you apart. One thing you can know for sure. Striving for harmony in the home is a good and Godly deed.

Wishing you a peaceful home,

Rabbi Daniel and Susan Lapin

6

2.
Guiding Your Children Through A Difficult Time

My husband and the father of my young twins, then age nine, died. How do I deal with the rebellion against God and me?

We never used foul language in our home, but now my eleven-year-old son and daughter use the worst of foul words repeatedly. Nothing I try seems to be working.

Sheri

Dear Sheri,

We read your letter with heavy hearts. What a difficult time for you and your children. Your children's behavior sounds more like a response to severe pain than a rebellion. We hope that you have a support system in place to help you with the many pragmatic and emotional difficulties you face as a widow.

You probably know that we have strong feelings about curse words, but in this case, we think the emphasis on language misses the larger picture. Your children may very well be angry with both God and you for "letting" their father die, and restoring a loving connection is first priority.

Please reach out for help to churches or other reputable organizations that work with grieving children. Your children need a safe environment in which to express themselves and meet others in similar circumstances. We know that you need to uphold standards in your house, but at the same time, please love your children harder and accept help in guiding them through this difficult period.

Sending prayers of encouragement,

Rabbi Daniel and Susan Lapin

3.
My Child Says He
Doesn't Believe in God

What response can I give my son when he states that he doesn't believe in God?

Roslyn

Dear Roslyn,

We imagine that this must be a painful question for you to ask. You didn't specify whether this is an adult son or a younger child, and the answer is different when you are dealing with a young adolescent, a teen on the verge of adulthood, or a full-grown man.

For the younger set, we think it is very important to make sure that parents don't turn a statement like this into a confrontation. Pre-teens and less mature teens (in some people this phase extends throughout their twenties) will often say statements deliberately to "get your goat." Other times, they are testing the waters and being provocative rather than deeply philosophical. In these cases, parents absolutely must exhibit more maturity than the child, which is easier said than done.

With younger as well as with older children, validating the individual's right to make their own decisions about God is necessary. This is something they will do with or without parental permission in any case. Separating from one's parents has to happen in order to have a relationship with God. Otherwise, one is simply "tagging on" to one's parents relationship.

Nevertheless, there is a difference between talking to a youngster or to an adult. Acknowledging the right for a child to hold his own views doesn't mean accepting behavior. Parents, for example, can tell a thirteen year old that his beliefs are his own but that, "In this family we go to church on Sunday." It is perfectly reasonable to tell a sixteen year old that while you appreciate hearing her views, it is not a conversation to have while her eight-year-old brother is around. The parents' tone of voice should be pleasant but firm while saying these things.

With a self-supporting adult child, parents can express preferences but not mandate behavior. You can be sympathetic to theological struggles while firm in your own convictions. If the child seems open and truly seeking then a parent can offer support such as help in finding people with whom to speak. However, at that stage of life, the best one can do is to retain an emotional connection with the child, make sure you are presenting a loving vision of God, and pray.

Keep a long-term perspective,

Rabbi Daniel and Susan Lapin

4.
Should I Use Logic or Emotion in Choosing a Mate?

A few weeks ago you spoke of marriage as being a contract based on devotion and reason as opposed to based on emotions like love.

What would you say to someone who believes he has found a woman who would make an excellent wife, yet he doesn't have those emotions for her, that chemistry? It seems a blessing because I can evaluate our compatibility more objectively, but at the same time, there is little driving me forward.

Brian

Dear Brian,

We're so glad you asked that question because we never want to minimize the importance of physical attraction and sexual chemistry in marriage. However, our society has it backwards, giving the message that physical attraction and chemistry should be the basis of the relationship and then devotion and reason should follow.

Sometimes, that happens. We do know of a number of situations where two individuals instantly "clicked" and entered into long and lasting marriages. But – and this is a big but – they often met in places, such as the home of friends or at a Bible study, where they quickly discovered that by being in that space, they had in effect been pre-vetted. They shared an outlook on God, life, and expectations for marriage and family so the physical attraction was in addition to other important factors.

Human beings are wired to be attracted to the familiar. If you aren't attracted to a woman whom you truly believe would make a great mate, we would strongly encourage you to give it a little time and see if she becomes more attractive to you as you get to know each other. You don't need to ask yourself, "Do I want to marry her?" but rather, "Was I more interested after this date than the previous one?" If the trajectory is moving upwards, keep on dating. There needs to be a balance between not wasting her (and your) time and leading her on, versus ending things too soon.

We carry the book, *I Only Want to Get Married Once: Dating Secrets for Getting it Right the First Time*, in our store because we think it does an excellent job in asking important questions that help singles separate infatuation from the potential for true and lasting commitment. The author, Chana Levitan, never minimizes the need for chemistry but does a wonderful job making sure that chemistry doesn't overrule everything else that matters.

We wish you success in finding your mate and building a home,

Rabbi Daniel and Susan Lapin

5.
Whose Job Is It To
Train Up the Children?

Whose job is it to train up the children? Mothers, fathers or both?

Debbie V.

Dear Debbie,

While our first thought was that we have no doubt that it is the responsibility and privilege of both mothers and fathers to train their children, we then realized that we need to support that conviction with Scripture.

Fortunately, King Solomon lays it out neatly for us in the book of Proverbs when he states, "Hear, my son, the discipline of your father and do not reject the teaching of your mother." While neither the word discipline nor the word teaching fully translate the Hebrew words used, the English does reveal that there are two distinct words.

Throughout the Bible, the importance of the family is maintained as well as the idea that men and women are naturally inclined to have differing sensitivities and ways of relating to all things, including their children.

While not every child is blessed with both mother and father, such as Benjamin whose mother Rachel died giving birth to him or Esther, who was orphaned, it is always important to know the ideal. Children need both mothering and fathering. Only if we know what the ideal is, can we compensate to the best of our ability when it isn't readily available.

Happy parenting,

Rabbi Daniel and Susan Lapin

6.
How Do We Know If We Are Enabling or Encouraging Our Adult Child?

I enjoy the Thought Tools and Susan's Musings each week and find they are worth reading over and over. Can you refer me to one of your books that would help me with my problem?

My husband and I are financially helping our adult son and daughter. We need to find a balance between encouragement and enabling. I'm happy to buy a book or any other advice you can give.

Pam

Dear Pam,

While we would love to encourage you to get all our re-sources, we don't have a specific one that deals with this is-sue. We would recommend looking around our friend, Dave Ramsey's website. He supplies practical, down-to-earth wis-dom on handling money. We're sure that some of his books would be helpful to you and your children.

The larger question at hand seems to be that the definition of adulthood has changed. It used to be that once a child reached a certain age, somewhere between the late teens and early twenties, he or she expected to be independent and took pride in that. While we may be going through tough economic times, they certainly aren't the toughest that have ever been. Rather, there has been a change in perception of both parent/child relationships and personal responsibility in general.

There are certainly individual circumstances that come into play, but our guess is that if you are worried about enabling your children, you are probably erring on the side of too much support. It isn't fair of us to shield our children from the realities of life when they are young. In the name of love, caring and kindness we often do our children a disservice by not allowing them to accept responsibility and forge good work and personal habits.

That said, if your children are actively and diligently pursuing an educational or other program providing a specific qualification that will enable them to acquire needed skills in a specific time period, your helping them might make sense. Such support could be linked to performance and industry. Even then, a frank discussion is in order.

We encourage you to explore this further, perhaps weaning your children off your support as you facilitate their becoming educated about how the world really works. Remember, just as you didn't let them eat all the candy they wanted or watch TV all day, by encouraging them to shoulder financial burdens you are not acting cruelly but rather taking your responsibility as parents seriously.

May you have much enjoyment from your adult children,

Rabbi Daniel and Susan Lapin

7.
Praying for a Future Mate

Is it okay to pray for a specific person to be your husband if that person is not already married?

Anonymous

Dear Anonymous,

Would it be all right with you if we substitute the word 'wise' for the word 'okay'? There is a principle that we have tried to follow in life. Don't tell a pro how to do his or her job. We don't go into a restaurant and hand the cook a recipe with detailed instructions on how to prepare our dinner. We pick the restaurant and our menu choice carefully and then look forward to the meal.

If we engage a plumber, a doctor or an accountant, we start with the assumption that the research we did to choose them was effective and that they know what they are doing. Now, with human beings, one always does have to keep one's critical faculties open. We have had the experience, for example, of getting in a taxi and discovering that we knew the route to our destination better than the 'expert' driver did.

With God, that worry falls away. So rather than tell God specifically whom you think is the right person for you, we think it would show more humility and faith to pray for God to let you meet the right person in a good and prompt time. You can add that if the person on whom your eye has fallen is the right one, you'd appreciate it becoming clear to you both. We further suggest constantly working on your own growth so that you are prepared for this major life step.

Happy praying,

Rabbi Daniel and Susan Lapin

8.
Is Marriage Necessary for Older Couples?

I am a senior citizen. I would like to know if it's necessary for older couples to marry before they live with each other.

Rebecca

Dear Rebecca,

We are delighted that you have found someone with whom you wish to share your life. Your question seems to presume either that a relationship that won't produce children or relationships of certain age groups might operate under a different set of rules. We assume you are asking us for an ancient Jewish wisdom perspective on this since, clearly, it is not necessary in today's culture or legal climate for couples to marry at all.

In addition to the very serious laws that govern adultery and other forbidden intimate relationships, there is a general concept of living in a sanctified manner (Lev. 19:2 among other places). We assume that you would like God's blessing on your life and it seems rather brazen to ask God to bless a relationship that is set up other than in His chosen manner – through marriage.

Furthermore, each one of us has an obligation to society in general. As we get older, our responsibility increases to set a proper example for those younger than we are. It is nice if a twenty year old serves as a role model, but it is expected for a seventy year old to do so. This is part of the Biblical compact that demands respect for elders (Lev. 19:32).

In a culture that downgrades the importance of marriage, it becomes especially vital for those of us who value it to actively promote and elevate marriage. Despite whatever added family, legal or tax burdens a marriage would entail, you and your beloved have an opportunity to strengthen society and honor God through your choice.

Wishing you health and happiness,

Rabbi Daniel and Susan Lapin

9.
What If One of Our Children Needs Less Support?

I have two sons. Jim is 18 and enlisted in the Marines last June. My other son Peter is 16 and still in high school. My wife and I opened college education accounts for the boys when they were young and both accounts have grown. Now that Jim is in the Marines, he intends to earn a college degree and have the U.S. military pay for it.

Assuming our government will make good on their promise to pay for Jim's education, and assuming our son Peter does not enlist in the military and wants to pursue a college degree, do you think my wife and I should take the cash in Jim's college education fund and give it to Peter for his education?

Jeff M.

Dear Jeff,

You are asking such an important question and one that, in one form or another, affects most families with more than one child. In its broader sense, the question is how to divide resources fairly among children.

If you don't mind, we are going to take a rather roundabout approach to answering your question. We would like to approach it from a few angles. Firstly, we think it is important for parents not to try to treat children as if they were all the same. If one child has frequent growth spurts and needs new shoes four times a year, while another can wear the same pair of shoes for twelve months, there is no need to worry about not being "fair" by purchasing more shoes for one than for the other. Similarly, not all children will want or benefit from art lessons, time at camp or other activities. Not giving exactly the same things to all is mandatory if one is correctly focused on each child's individual needs. All children need love; they do not all need the same treatment or objects.

However - and this is a big however - we need to take a lesson from Jacob and the serious problems which were caused when his sons felt that he favored one of them—Joseph—over all the others. Most children, no matter how wrong they are, will decide at one point or another that Mom and Dad have a favorite child. At times one child will need to get way more things or attention than another. However, Mom and Dad need to monitor their actions, reactions and time and money distribution to make sure that they are acting in a fashion which is not necessarily fair in the short term, but which is fair in the overall picture.

Let's meld these two ideas in your situation. You responsibly set aside money so that you could give your sons a college education, and one of them has made that action unnecessary, because of a meritorious and commendable choice that he made to serve his country. In a case like this, we think a point that our (Rabbi Lapin's) father made to us when we had a houseful of small children is on the mark. He urged us to make a will, but advised us not to name any individuals as our choice for raising our children should something happen to us. What Rabbi Lapin (Sr.) suggested was that we instead name the people whom we would trust to make that decision for us if the time ever came, and to have a frank conversation with them about what we most valued plus any reservations we might have about obvious alternatives. He told us that life isn't static and if the day arrived when our children needed a new home, the decision would need to be made with the facts available at the time. All sorts of unforeseen things could make a couple who we might think of as best for our children unable to take them in or no longer the people we would wish to raise the children. We took his advice, which, thank God, never needed to be used.

In your case, our guess is that you are thinking of a college education as shorthand for wanting to give your sons a leg up in life. Jim may not need that specific leg up, but he may very well need money to start a business, explore a less traditional path than college or for an unforeseen circumstance. The money in his account could be his opportunity to establish a successful life for himself. If you give it away, you would, in effect, be penalizing him for his decision to join the Marines.

Not only might you regret this decision down the road, but you might damage the relationship between your sons. We hope that both of your boys feel a responsibility to watch over and help each other and strengthening their bond will be more valuable to both Jim and Peter than any monetary assistance you can give them.

We wish you and your boys lives of blessing, health and abundance.

Rabbi Daniel and Susan Lapin

10.
Keeping Children Occupied
Without Television

In one of your TV shows, Susan mentioned that you don't own a television. As the father of 9, I wanted to know how you kept your children occupied without at least the ability to watch good quality family entertainment.

Mark H.

Mark,

We have never tried to prioritize our top ten parenting tips, but if we did, not having a television would probably rank right up there. Without TV, our kids made their own entertainment. Having a full house meant there were always companions around. In addition to the thousands of books they devoured, they were constantly using their imaginations (along with furniture, construction toys and everything else in the house) to sail off to foreign shores, set up businesses and practice army maneuvers. The dark secret of TV is that it stifles imagination. The more you watch, the less capable you become of filling hours without it.

From a very young age, our children were a vital part of running our home. They became competent in the kitchen at young ages, did their own laundry and helped in all sorts of ways. While we occasionally heard rumblings about chores, our children knew better than to utter the words, "I'm bored." We were only too happy to hear that as there were always dishes that needed washing, floors that needed mopping and long lists of other jobs that had not yet been assigned. They also spent a great deal of time running enterprises such as lemonade stands and offering various services to neighbors.

We did sometimes watch videos, a practice that started when six of the children had chicken pox. We showed them *Mary Poppins* over the course of three nights, allowing Susan a chance to make dinner and have a break from the 'Mommy Camp' she was running for the invalids. For many years after that, videos were a rare activity which we watched together as a family. Sometimes the younger ones watched a *Winnie the Pooh* type video and then went to bed while the older family members saw more advanced fare. But solitary watching almost never happened unless someone was sick and needed to be isolated. To our regret, as our older children grew, watching videos with friends became a more frequent pastime for Saturday nights. In retrospect, we wish we would have limited that time even more.

Today, the challenge is far greater with movies and TV shows instantly accessible via computer and smart phones. But the principle still holds that passively watching electronic entertainment is one of the least productive uses of time and the more you watch the less creative you are.

If TV and video watching is already part of your life, eliminating it or cutting down on the hours will be a painful process. If you can endure the transition, the results are well worth it.

Rabbi Daniel and Susan Lapin

11.
Can I Protect My Children from Prejudice?

I am an African American woman raising children in a rural part of America. My children have received some negative interactions / insults from their peers in regards to their skin color. I am torn as to how appropriately respond to these attacks against my family. I am quite angered by these insults but I do not wish to cultivate hatred in my children. Do you have any biblical insights on how to deal with this infuriating issue? I cannot allow my children to endure harassment without a swift and thoughtful response on my part.

Dear Anna,

Don't we all wish we could shield our children from negative interactions and insults? It is painful to watch them suffer and we commend you for realizing that your response can affect them even more than the incidents themselves.

We are quite sure that many of our readers have suggestions to make based on their own experiences. We would like to offer three thoughts but we recognize that they are certainly not a complete answer.

> 1) Most importantly, you along with relatives, teachers, neighbors, pastors and others can constantly reinforce in your children the idea that they are created in God's image as unique and valued individuals with huge potential. If they are secure in your love and the love of

others, the negative statements will not pierce them as they will if that cushion is not there. Treat them with empathy, rather than with anger or pity. Your children need to see that those who taunt them are reflecting badly on themselves rather than making accurate statements about their victims.

2) Have your children read histories of figures like Dr. Ben Carson, Thomas Sowell and Judge Clarence Thomas as well as historical figures like Harriet Tubman, Frederick Douglas and Booker T. Washington. Have them become familiar with broader history, too. If they only learn of discrimination against the Black community, you run the risk that they see themselves as aggrieved victims. Victimhood is difficult to overcome. They should learn how other groups have been discriminated against, such as the Jewish people; Irish, Japanese and Chinese immigrants to America; the Armenian massacre and so forth. Stories of persecution are, sadly, not hard to find.

3) It is worth exploring whether the comments made to your children are unique, or if the culture you live in is one of insult, be it making fun of braces, glasses, high or low grades, a lack of athletic ability or myriad other potential opportunities for mockery. Inculcate respect and compassion for others in your children. Too often the bullied become the bullies when the opportunity presents itself. Inoculate your children against this by building their self-respect (rather than meaningless self-esteem). Hold them to a high standard of behavior and achievement and celebrate when they meet those standards. Make sure they have opportunities to be givers, whether it is visiting an old-age home, earning money and donating to charity or helping a neighbor in need.

The above suggestions only reflect on your interaction with your children. It is very possible that you can and should speak to their teachers and/or the parents of some of these children. You need to monitor the situation to know whether direct adult intervention is needed or if some 'behind the scenes' wisdom can be applied, perhaps working on getting to know the other children as individuals.

We wish you success in raising a confident family full of love for God and for all His children,

Rabbi Daniel and Susan Lapin

12.
Honoring Your Father and Mother When They Are Less Than Honorable

Recently in our study group, I suggested that we could do away with the legal overload in Congress if all we did was to follow the Ten Commandments.

One of the women present asked how one could keep the commandment to 'Honor thy mother and thy father' if one had abusive parents.

Can you shed light on this?

Fred G.

Dear Fred,

If you have listened to our audio CD, *The Ten Command-ments*, you already know that those 'commandments' are actually ten statements which encapsulate man's relationship with God and with his fellow man. Each one is a stepping-stone to the next level of interaction.

The oral transmission of ancient Jewish wisdom since Sinai fills in the areas where a perfect law intersects with imperfect people. Ideally, all parents would be loving and competent; unfortunately this is not so in reality. There is an exquisite tension balancing adherence to an absolute standard with functioning in the real world. One could technically observe the entire Torah and yet be considered disgusting in God's eyes because of the spirit in which one does so. Conversely, one could be beloved in God's eyes though not meticulous in observance. God will judge us all by His own measures.

The fact that some parents fall extraordinarily far from the ideal is a problem, but not a good reason to abolish the unique relationship between parents and children as some socialist experiments encouraged. A case could be made that all children should be raised in scrupulously regulated government institutions because some children are abused and even killed by their parents. Yet, almost everyone understands that more children would suffer under institutional conditions, not fewer. As a society, we should safeguard the parent/child relationship while doing what we can to protect individual, unfortunate children.

Judaism resolves this paradox by commanding everyone to honor his or her parents. But 'honoring' is a specific way of behaving; it is not decided by each person's own conscience or desire. There are times when one is obligated not to follow a parent's wishes, for example if a parent would tell a child not to marry so that he is better able to care for that parent. Having abusive parents doesn't nullify the commandment, however it affects in what way that 'honoring' is carried out.

We would not say that the Ten Commandments at face value are enough to guide a society. However, we can be sure that running a society without being guided by them is a sure recipe for certain failure.

Rabbi Daniel and Susan Lapin

13.
Helping a Child Who Is Making Poor Choices

My 33 year old son - a really good person - always seems to select the wrong person as a possible future mate. Something always seems to go dreadfully wrong and he ends up being hurt and rejected.

Can you please give some advice as to what could possibly be going wrong?

Thank you,

N.

Dear N.,

It is incredibly painful for parents to watch their children hurting. We want to "kiss it better" as we did when they took a tumble as toddlers, but, alas, that method no longer works.

You are recognizing a pattern in your son's relationships, which most likely does mean that he is repeating some mistaken behavior. Unfortunately, he needs to be the one who wants to examine his thoughts and actions. You can't figure this one out for him and even if you did it is useless unless he chooses to pay attention.

Perhaps the best help you can give, aside from loving him,

is to present the idea that dating and marriage are not areas in which we instinctively know how to act. You might want to browse your local bookstore or library and see if there are books from which your son could benefit. You could buy them as a gift or simply have them around when he visits. We humbly suggest our audio CD, *Madam, I'm Adam*, which extracts Bible information showing that we are not born instinctively knowing how to build a male/female relationship any more than we are born instinctively knowing how to bake soufflés or dance ballet.

Help him with these steps: (1) First, find out if he is willing to discuss it with you. If not, there is no point in wasting your time and jeopardizing your relationship with him. (2) If he is willing to talk, ask him if he recognizes his historic pattern. (3) If he does, ask him if he considers it coincidence or if it could be due to something he is doing. (4) Gently probe with questions that can help him see himself more clearly. Note: Make no declarative statements; only ask questions.

The bottom line is that you can be a resource and source of support for your son, but he will need to do the hard work of accessing the truth on his own.

Rabbi Daniel and Susan Lapin

14.
Ideal Husband and Wife Roles
When Earning a Living

My husband wants us to read your book, Thou Shall Prosper. Does the book include what the wife's role is in the family?

Thanks,

Mary

Dear Mary,

We have always believed that once you move past adolescent jobs and into adult ones, there is no such thing as a one person job. Major corporations used to understand this and they never hired someone for a senior management position without interviewing the wife as well. They were looking to see if the man would have support in the home so that he could do his job.

This is no longer politically correct nor representative of the workforce, but it doesn't mean that each working person can function on his (or her) own. We firmly believe that one of the reasons that the American family is under so much stress is because our society encouraged women into the workplace without expecting or preparing for any negative consequences.

While we personally think that for the majority of couples, it is better if the husband is responsible for earning the living, for the sake of this analysis it doesn't matter. Two people working full time means that no one has support. Even if there is enough money (which there usually isn't) to hire a full range of helpers to cook, clean, run errands and manage the house, someone who is out in the workplace every day needs emotional and social back-up. We're not even discussing taking care of children, which demands a parent's participation. Expecting a marriage and family to thrive while both husband and wife spend tremendous time and energy working independently is naïve.

Ideally, we should think in terms of a job belonging to a married couple. If they are fortunate enough to function with only one paycheck, that check is earned by both of them. We hope that reading *Thou Shall Prosper* together and absorbing the mind set it advocates will help you function as one unit.

Happy teamwork,

Rabbi Daniel and Susan Lapin

15.
I Think My Husband and I
Are Unequally Yoked

What does the Jewish faith teach on being unequally yoked and divorce? After much counseling and maturing, I now see how unequally yoked I am with my husband. I feel that I married him before I knew myself and realize he is very manipulative and verbally abusive.

Thank you for your response!

Mary M.

Dear Mary,

While the Jewish, Catholic and Protestant religions may have different views about whether there is any place for divorce in human interaction, the three share a concept of marriage as something holy.

While divorce is allowed in Judaism, it is not treated lightly or casually. Divorce should be considered only after every other option is exhausted. Not knowing you, we certainly can't comment on your specific marriage, however we can make some general comments.

It is very easy to be caught up in the divorce culture that pervades our current times. Too many counselors and psychologists, let alone women's support groups, push women to leave their marriages. Without minimizing how extreme verbal abuse can be, it does not have a clear definition. Neither does the word "manipulative".

In a Jewish world-view, divorce is sometimes, tragically, necessary. However, there are untold couples who celebrate 50th anniversaries, surrounded by children and grandchildren, because they worked through problems rather than abandoning the marriage. Having said that, there have been extreme cases where we have counseled divorce when we saw that as the only way for an individual (and sometimes the children involved) to have a chance for a healthy life.

We would encourage you to assemble a support team who will give you Godly, wise and practical guidance. Make sure the members of this team value marriage at the same time as they have experience with the real world. If there is any chance that your husband and you can grow and change together, you need to work hard to make that happen. If there are children involved, your decision is even weightier.

Should a divorce be the only viable alternative, and if it is allowed in your faith, knowing you have done all in your power to avoid that occurrence will allow you to move forward with a clear conscience and untroubled soul.

Stay strong,

Rabbi Daniel and Susan Lapin

16.
At What Age is it O.K.
to Defy Parents?

A friend of ours says that the Biblical evidence is that a young man becomes an adult at age 20 and his parents no longer have authority over him. He is using this argument to justify his own defiance of his father.

Is this Biblical, and is there any Biblical evidence for a situation in which a child would defy his parents (excepting, of course, a situation in which a clear Biblical commandment is at stake)?

Thank you,

Hannah H.

Dear Hannah,

The language you use in your email – "defy" "authority", "justify"- suggests that something is amiss in the way your friend is thinking.

"Honor your father and mother" doesn't expire no matter how old you get. So "defying" parents never becomes all right. At the same time, as one grows, there is sometimes a conflict of obligations. As you mention, sometimes parents demand that a child rejects God's commands. A number of our students through the years had to explain to their parents that as they accepted religious obligations like keeping the Sabbath, they weren't able to answer their parents' phone calls on Saturday or drive over to their houses.

We find it interesting that Jewish transmission specifically states that honoring parents does not include an obligation to marry someone that your parent chooses for you.

Sometimes a choice has to be made between an obligation to a spouse and an obligation to parents. Other times there is a conflict between responsibilities to one's own children or business and to one's parents. However, that isn't defiance, but a question of not being able to fulfill two conflicting needs at one time.

Ancient Jewish wisdom stresses the importance of having a personal religious guide who can help navigate confusing and conflicting situations like these, with full understanding of the specific circumstances and individuals involved. Actively seeking a wise mentor is a piece of advice that is useful for people of all religions. In this case, a mentor might help your friend do the right thing rather than justify a wrong choice.

Rabbi Daniel and Susan Lapin

17.
My Child's Spouse is Rude and Disrespectful!

My daughter dated a man that my husband and I hardly ever met. She ended up marrying him. After two years of marriage, they have two daughters.

He has been rude and disrespectful to us this whole season of knowing him. He has made it clear that he does not want us in his home.

What do we do as parents?

Trudy W.

Dear Trudy,

We are sorry that you and your husband are in such a painful situation. At this point, you are concerned about not only your relationship with your daughter, but also about what sort of relationship you will have with your granddaughters.

Without knowing any more than what you wrote, it sounds as if there was somewhat of an estrangement from your daughter before her marriage, since you weren't heavily involved in her choice of husband. We don't know if this was unique to this particular man or not. Does his negative reaction to you stem from how you felt about him or is his rudeness based on something else?

Either way, there is now a fait accompli. Your daughter is married and building a family with her husband. Unless she is unhappy with the situation and approaches you for help, your only choice is to accept the situation and take the initiative to end all negativity. We would suggest taking small steps such as offering to babysit or to drop off something you have cooked. You can also send cards for different occasions, including their anniversary. In other words, you need to keep on taking baby steps forward without expecting anything in return. Just hope and pray that your love will penetrate the fence your daughter and son-in-law have erected.

You cannot change whatever happened in the past. However, you don't need to limit your future by being unwilling to move forward. Keep in mind that your goal is not to oppose your son-in-law but to be part of your daughter and granddaughters' lives.

Keep the end goal in mind,

Rabbi Daniel and Susan Lapin

18.
Marrying Someone from a Different Faith

I have been a Christian for 5 years now. I recently met a man who is Muslim. We are very much in love and want to get married, but everyone in my church (including family) tell me he is not for me because of his religion.

I know the Bible says not to be yoked with unbelievers, but this person very much loves God as well. And to be honest, I have met people from other religions who are much 'nicer' than Christians, if you know what I mean.

Please give me your advice.

Karla D

Dear Karla,

As the parents of six daughters, one phrase in your email sends shivers up our spine. It is, "we are very much in love." We're sure you agree that the vast majority of people who get married are "very much in love," yet the divorce rate, as well as the many people living unhappily married lives, suggests that being in love is a poor reason to get married. As easily as love grows, it can die. Marriage is about commitment and action, not emotion.

A marriage can be successful when one person like Italian food and the other likes Mexican; when one spouse likes baseball and it bores the other to tears. But either religion means something or it doesn't. If religion matters, it is your window to the truth.

No nationality, religion, race or gender is made up only of wonderful people. That there are people professing to be Christians who don't live up to the ideals of Christianity is irrelevant. Whether your friend is a wonderful person is irrelevant also. What matters is what underlying framework will be the basis for every decision in your life.

Our advice would be to recognize that you are in the grip of an emotion and surround yourself with support to protect yourself from acting on that emotion. If that isn't something you choose to do, then we recommend that you learn as much as possible about Islam from outside sources – not from your boyfriend. The Internet is a wonderful doorway to knowledge. Make sure you read negative as well as positive sources.

If his family is from another country, we suggest you visit that country – and not with him. Unless both of you are willing to openly and publicly renounce your faith or one of you wholeheartedly converts, then we think that moving forward would be short sighted and potentially the source of more unhappiness than you can begin to imagine.

Rabbi Daniel and Susan Lapin

19.
Using Scripture to Rationalize Wrong Behavior

A family member is living with someone. He says according to the Old Testament that he is married. He uses the example of when Isaac went "into" Rebecca. There was no wedding ceremony, just a consummation. I am very interested to know your answer to this.

Pat K.

Dear Pat,

Isn't it amazing how we human beings can rationalize all sorts of behavior that deep down we know are wrong?

Genesis 24:67 actually says, "And Isaac brought her into the tent of his mother, Sarah, and he took Rebecca and she was a wife to him..."

Why do we suspect that your friend, who seems intent on following every word, didn't take his female acquaintance into his mother's tent?

If you have learned anything from our teachings, you know that a surface reading of the Bible reveals little. Doesn't this verse seem a bit ghoulish? Isaac isn't taking Rebecca to meet his mother; Sarah is already dead. Like many Hebrew words, the word "ohel" or tent has a deeper meaning. In our case,

Isaac is explaining his worldview and that of his parents, to Rebecca. After she agrees that she wishes to live her life by the same principles as Sarah lived hers, he marries her. The Hebrew verb in that verse means, "taking as a wife," and accepting all the lifetime responsibilities, financial and otherwise that the act entails. After that "taking" if something went very wrong, a divorce would be necessary to end the relationship.

In our society, living with someone in no way means making a lifetime commitment of shared values with divorce being the only means to end the relationship. We don't think that you should be influenced by your friend's words into thinking that he is behaving in an upright and correct manner.

Rabbi Daniel and Susan Lapin

20.
Generational Curses:
Can We Start Over?

The Bible speaks of generational curses. If such a curse exists in one's life, is there a way to get this removed?

Bill F.

Dear Bill,

We appreciate your asking this question as we are sure many people find the idea of generational curses difficult to swallow. Why would a loving God saddle a newborn with the sins of his father?

Let us start by pointing out that God does us a gracious service by describing the world He has built. Understanding the rules allows us to make wise choices. The truth is that each child who enters this world is not a blank slate. He receives a genetic and spiritual inheritance. If someone's parent and grandparent have a history of heart disease, he probably is more likely to be prone to the same malady than someone from a healthier background. Knowing of this weakness allows him to be proactive in countering the tendency.

Similarly, a child born into a loving and stable family does have an advantage over the offspring of a single, cocaine addicted mother. We can yell, "It's not fair," all we like, but it would be smarter to use our efforts to promote marriage and healthy living than to protest.

In telling us of generational curses, God is letting us know that our actions affect more than our own lives. What we do, the choices we make, are going to influence our children. Many of us would rather takes risks with our own lives, than potentially harm our descendants. Even teenagers and young adults would behave differently if they truly understood that reality, instead of getting the false message from society that all they need to think about is their own fulfillment and living their own lives.

A person can do something of such spiritual import that it will reverberate through the generations, putting his descendants at a disadvantage. What is also true, however, is that each individual has free choice and with great effort, can move himself out of one sphere of influence and into another. In short, there are spiritual processes we can use to make ourselves into an entirely new person.

The idea of generational curses may seem callous at first, but, with contemplation, we can see that it describes reality and makes each one of us into a person of great value and importance.

Rabbi Daniel and Susan Lapin

21.
Is There a Place for Singles in Religious Life?

I am single lady in my forties desiring to be married. I have tried to live a life that would please God. My church doesn't do anything to help someone like me and I am beginning to feel left out and ignored from all social aspects in the church.

What else can I do besides praying about this matter?

Betthany

Dear Betthany,

We have heard similar statements from older singles in synagogues as well. So much of religious life circles around couples and families. Those who don't fit either of those categories often feel left out.

You should feel proud that you have tried to "live a life that would please God" despite the challenges that come with not finding a life-mate.

We hope you have learned to function with two competing visions at all times: 1) Living a fulfilling single life 2) Behaving in a way that opens up the opportunity for marriage. Achieving both those aims at the same time is difficult and might take you out of your comfort zone. For example, you may find that the church you are in answers your spiritual needs, filling condition one, but doesn't expose you to new men or actively promote ways to help you move towards marriage. This could mean that you need to spend time at other churches or volunteer for organizations that can provide new interactions. Many organizations and volunteer opportunities attract decent and faithful individuals.

You might also wish to look for a loving and honest 'marriage mentor' whether in your church or elsewhere who can help you present yourself in a more positive light. In addition, you should actively seek friendships with married couples whose relationships you see as a model for your own future marriage.

If you are excluded from classes at your church that are open only to couples, perhaps you could suggest new ideas for classes that would attract a broader base. In your email, you mentioned a discomfort with approaching your pastor on this issue due to events in her own life. Perhaps you are misjudging her or perhaps this is a prod for you to seek another faith leader.

We know you are not discounting the value of prayer, but God does expect action as well. We would suggest giving yourself the task of trying three new ways this month to 'shake up' your life in this area and then evaluate them. Giving yourself specific tasks will help you to feel proactive and energize you. This can only benefit you whether you are blessed with finding your mate or if you continue carving out a productive, Godly life on your own.

Rabbi Daniel and Susan Lapin

22.
What are the Most Important Things to Remember When Getting Married?

I am getting married to a wonderful young lady in just under two months! We just finished our pre-marital counseling at our church, and are finishing the preparations for the "Big Day".

I know that marriage, and making it work well, is more than the feel good emotions and so on, even though they are very nice... :) So my question is, what are a few of the most important things that I should keep in mind, and do, to have a successful and enjoyable marriage?

David S.

Dear David,

We want to respond with information different from what you probably already know (i.e. respect each other in front of other people) or what one of your bride's magazines might suggest (i.e. set regular date times).

For brevity, we're going to narrow our answer to only one important thing. We suggest asking yourself on a daily basis: "What could I do today to enhance my marriage?"

Marriage is a living organism, which means that it is always in a state of change. It is growing and getting better or it is shrinking and decaying. Just as a person's heartbeat is reflected on an EKG as waves, with peaks and valleys, the life of a marriage will be reflected in its ups and downs. That means the marriage is alive. To thrive, the highs need to be more frequent and more intense than the occasional lows.

One of the most powerful ways we know to inject vitality into the marriage is to make sure that not only is each of you growing as an individual, but that you delight in each other's growth. You also need to make time to have ample growth together. Our favorite way of doing this is to share meaningful Bible study on a regular basis. Veering off a sailing course by only one or two degrees may seem like a small matter, but over the course of weeks will have you missing landfall. Similarly, it is easy in a marriage for there to be small, seemingly insignificant changes, which down the road prove to be major obstacles in the relationship. Studying God's word together in a meaningful way will make sure that you are constantly recalibrating your course together.

Wishing you all the best,

Rabbi Daniel and Susan Lapin

23.
My Husband Wants Me
to Get a Job

Thank you for giving me this space to help me clarify my thoughts. My husband has a good job; he is an excellent provider. I am a good wife; I take care of him and our two little ones. He works in a job that needs him to travel every week.

I consider we are a good team. He works and provides. I stay home and take care of everything else.

The problem is when he asks me to go to work. He tells me all the time that I need to be out of the nest. He puts money in my night table every week. I don't have a credit card or checking account. He says that we are fine like this. I don't agree. I am the kind of woman that shops with coupons and looks for clearance sales. He doesn't appreciate the way I contribute to the family.

I feel very hurt when he pushes me too hard to go to work even though he has a good job. If he is not here during the week and I will be outside working, who is going to take care of our girls?

Please help. Thanks!

Gabriela

Dear Gabriela,

You are raising an issue to which many couples can relate. While you see the two of you as a good team, for a team to work well together each member of the team needs to appreciate the contributions of the other. It doesn't sound to us like you and your husband are reading from the same playbook.

We understand you are feeling hurt, but you need to put aside your feelings and have a non-emotional conversation with your husband. Ask him to explain why he wants you to go to work. Is he worried that in this economy his job might be at risk and feeling tremendous pressure that he is the sole breadwinner? Does he feel that when you have time together you only want to talk about the children and he wants your horizons to expand so that he can enjoy being with the fascinating woman he married? Did his upbringing expose him to women who stayed home and watched soap operas all afternoon, so that he doesn't value a hands-on mother and homemaker? Does he have a relationship with your daughters so that he can appreciate how much work is involved with caring properly for children? You need to understand the reasons he wants you to work before you can tackle this issue.

This discussion also needs to include a talk about finances. The way things are now, with you being shut out of your financial life, is not a sustainable model. It doesn't sound as if you are working as partners in any area of your marriage.

We would strongly advise the two of you to have outside help in facilitating this conversation. It is so important that the many talks you need to have don't devolve into tears, recriminations and anger, and instead become a step towards truly functioning as a team. One idea that we have seen work for many is finding a mentor couple that is trained to help younger couples negotiate through difficult issues. A good marriage counselor could be very helpful, but you have to very careful to find one who values marriage vows. Some marriage counselors may have a different agenda. The effort that goes towards finding the right person or people to work with the two of you will be paid back many times over.

There is little as rewarding as being a member of a real marriage partnership. Your daughters will benefit as well if you and your husband work towards that goal.

We wish you success and look forward to hearing from you as you progress in your efforts,

Rabbi Daniel and Susan Lapin

24.
What's the Biblical View on Interracial Marriage?

Is it unbiblical to marry outside of one's race?

Our daughter and her African American friend approached my wife and I and asked if it would bother us if they started seeing each other. Meaning...testing the spirit and seeing if God is possibly placing them together as a couple and eventually marriage. We are Caucasian. Actually I have Cherokee Indian and German in my blood. Both my daughter and the young African American are very sincere about this relationship. They both honored us by asking how we viewed their relationship. My daughter is 29 and the young man is 30.

Thank you for your input.

Rick

Dear Rick,

What a wonderful relationship you must have with your daughter for this young couple to want input from you and your wife!

We have discussed this issue regarding our own children, though it has been a theoretical rather than practical discussion as it is for you. Let us share our thoughts with you.

One of the reasons we feel that it is so important to know

that God created each individual and that there is a spiritual as well as a physical world is that it leads naturally to focusing less on the material externals of people. If we are raising flowers or sheep, then the coloring, shape and other features matter a great deal. But if the external parts of a person are of less importance than his or her character and soul, then unless one is screening someone for a job as a fashion model, those things should matter less.

We do not believe that God intends us to choose marriage partners based on race. In fact, Jewish tradition tells us that Moses married a black woman.

With that said, we have also discussed that should we be faced with such a situation, we would want to make sure that our child understood as much as possible what reactions to such a match might be, for future offspring as well as for the couple themselves. This is exactly how we would feel if our children wanted to marry someone from another country or markedly different social or economic background. In other words, realistically assessing a situation is a sign of maturity.

Considering that both your daughter and her friend are survivors of previous marriages, their ages, and the fact that you know this young man for a number of years, our guess is that they have the maturity and commitment to explore this relationship with God's blessing.

Rabbi Daniel and Susan Lapin

25.
Teen Interracial Dating

Teen interracial dating, Different color - same religion.

Is it right or wrong?

Pete W.

You are a man of few words, Pete. However, we'd like to focus on only one word out of your question – the word "teen." We have discussed interracial marriage in a previous 'Ask the Rabbi.' Teen dating is another issue entirely.

The teenage years are ones of precious opportunity to help our children prepare for being adults. It is a time in which to become confident in and aware of one's own individual talents. These are years for strengthening one's character and learning to interact with many different people.

Dating during this time limits and distorts one's perspective. We can think of little that can hinder mature growth more than prematurely focusing on one person with whom to have a relationship. In our hyper-sexualized society it also thrusts young people into situations for which very few are prepared.

Our advice for parents with young children is to build a family and social group where dating will not be part of the paradigm for your children as they become teenagers. By the time your children are ready to court - and that is not the same thing as dating - they should have a pretty good picture of what they are looking for in a marriage partner and be ready to move a relationship forward towards that end.

Rabbi Daniel and Susan Lapin

26.
Will God Forgive Me for My Live-in Boyfriend?

I am a divorced mother of two who lives with my boyfriend and children. Will this keep me from going to heaven?

Lynn

Dear Lynn,

As Orthodox Jews who are mere mortals, we do not presume to speak for God. We believe that after death there is a reckoning of all we have done during our time on earth, but accept that God, with His omniscient wisdom, may assess things differently than you or we do. Nonetheless, we think we do best when we follow His blueprint.

We hope that you will focus on what you are doing in this world while you are still alive. We are sure that your divorce was painful and that you are well aware that your children have a harder path to hoe growing up in a home without a mother and father. We're also sure that you want to do everything you can to help your children succeed.

We do believe you should examine your actions, perhaps with the help of a trusted mentor, and ask if by bringing a boyfriend into your home you are stumbling in your primary responsibility to your children. Statistically, living in a home with a mother's boyfriend does not bode well for children.

Even if your boyfriend is a wonderful man and your relationship is a lasting one, possibly even turning into marriage, are you giving your children a message of morality and responsibility or teaching them to ignore what is right in favor of what is, in the short term, desirable?

By asking the question that you did, we think you know the answer to our question. There are support groups for single mothers in churches around the country, and we urge you to take advantage of those places where you can be helped to live the healthiest life, physically and spiritually, for both yourself and your children.

Best wishes,

Rabbi Daniel and Susan Lapin

27.
Why Do Innocent People Suffer?

How does God see special needs children and, what is His purpose for them here on earth? I am a mother of twin boys with autism.

Thank you,

Mayme M.

Dear Mayme,

In the broadest sense you are asking why innocent people suffer, and that millennia-old question can truly only be answered by God, in His own time. However, we would like to offer two ways of thinking that we hope will be a source of strength to you.

First of all, we see only two ways of looking at babies born with disabilities, be they physical, emotional or mental. Either this is a random occurrence – just the luck of the draw – or there is a Planner guiding the world who cares about each and every newborn. While knowing that God is in control may initially lead to anger and struggling with Him, we think that, overall, it is a comforting thought. While the reason for the suffering may be beyond our comprehension, there is a reason understood by One greater than us when things don't go as we hoped and prayed they would.

If we accept the belief that events are not random, we can

then be assured that each soul has its own mission to accomplish on this earth. Every soul is given precisely the tools it needs to do its job. Furthermore, each child, wherever on the spectrum of health he or she may fall, is given to a mother and father to help the parents complete their jobs in this world as well.

Internalizing this idea is a pretty lofty aspiration and being human, we frequently don't do the best job we could. Even when we fail, we have the chance to try again, and we do believe that God is cheering us on.

You surely have days where you simply cannot see how you can be patient and loving for one more minute. There is a constant pain at seeing your twin boys struggle with things that most children take for granted. We pray that God gives you glimpses into the value of your sons' lives and the ways in which their challenges can help you become greater than you are.

Sending virtual hugs,

Rabbi Daniel and Susan Lapin

Questions & Answers
About Finances

28.
How Can I Get Around Impediments to My Success?

I recently attended your talk in the United Kingdom and your talk further inspired me to realize financial success. I have looked for gaps in the service market -- to no avail. I am a married woman of medium intelligence and tenacity but feel hemmed in and unsure as to what I can achieve at my age (53 yrs).

Can you advise what to do?

Glenis S.

Dear Glenis,

I am delighted that you attended one of my talks in the United Kingdom. I delivered 20 speeches during my visit and I found each one exhilarating because of the many wonderful people I met. Your letter refers to one of the central ideas we teach – that you should look to fill a need of your fellow humans, and that finding and filling those needs will bring financial success.

Obviously, we cannot give you individual advice. You have your own unique talents and resources. You might explore going for competent career counseling or finding other ways of expanding your outlook. Perhaps you can try a number of volunteer activities or offer to intern somewhere to become familiar with a new field. Without knowing more about you and your circumstances, our practical advice is, of necessity, limited.

One thing we can tell you, though, is that you must overcome the mental block that says the words, "at my age." Sam Walton was about your age when he got retailing giant Walmart going. Colonel Harland Sanders was much older than you when he started Kentucky Fried Chicken. It is important not to confuse reality with excuses. Each one of us is a master at explaining why we can't succeed. Whether it is our age, nationality, gender, physical limitations, etc., etc., etc., everyone has some external fact that we can use to tell ourselves why it is futile to strive or try.

This isn't to say that impediments don't exist. They do. However, successful individuals find ways around impediments or they forge new paths that avoid them. While we are sorry that we can't offer you concrete career advice, we can tell you that reminding yourself how energetic, competent and hardworking you are (and work on becoming those things if you suspect you might not be) is the first step you need to take.

Finally, make it a point to meet and befriend three new people every week. As your social circle expands, keep asking people what needs they have or see around them that you could help with. These discussions will evolve into brainstorming sessions that may yield the answer to the question about which you wrote to us.

Let us know how things go,

Rabbi Daniel and Susan Lapin

29.
Is There a Spiritual
Dimension to Money?

The Bible asks us not to serve two masters: God and Mammon. I was startled to hear you speak about a spiritual dimension to money. While most religions view money devoid of spirituality, what is your justification? Please throw some light.

Subash

Subash,

The Torah instructs us not to serve any god other than God, and we can only reply to you using that as our starting point rather than the quote you are referencing. This instruction suggests that for each individual and collectively in different times and places, any variety of gods may arise. Money can certainly be one, as can academic achievement, environmentalism, humanism or any other pursuit which we put ahead of following God.

You're asking us to sum up in a few words a central thesis of our book, *Thou Shall Prosper: The Ten Commandments for Making Money*. We go into great detail there as to why money is spiritual rather than physical. We also define the meaning of spiritual and point out that all spiritual things can be used by people for good or for evil.

We would be doing you a terrible disservice if we tried to cover this topic that rapidly in the 'Ask the Rabbi' format.

However, here is a question to get you started on what seems to be a new way of thinking for you. Do you think that God smiles on the use of money in human interaction or would He be happier if currency was non-existent?

Happy exploration,

Rabbi Daniel and Susan Lapin

30.
How Can I Keep My Sanity
When it Comes to Money?

I met you at Nessah Synagogue. I was very touched by your speech in regards to money and marriage. How can I, as a wife and mother of four, guide this "liquid" to pour more easily onto my family?

Times are tough and my husband is the only one working now. We have encountered many financial challenges in the past few years and I can't see the light at the end of the tunnel. The kids are growing and the expenses are high.

How can I keep my faith and sanity when it comes to money? I have a hard time being focused and positive. The chaos happening around the world is not helping my psyche as well. I am looking for some sort of security and relief at this point.

Looking forward to your reply and all the best,

Nikki

Nikki,

We are sure that many people can relate to the feelings you express. If your family was struggling financially while the economy was good and jobs were readily available your question would be a different one. However, in today's world, where the entire economy is struggling, you aren't asking for practical advice as much as for an approach to help you handle this difficult time. As you say, with chaos around the world in addition to personal financial stress, it is easy to feel overwhelmed and powerless.

Perhaps there are ways you can supplement your family's income or help your husband to market his skills more effectively. You should certainly not ignore taking steps that can be implemented. But you are asking about the psychological arena and there are things you need to do to help your family get through this period.

You are particularly asking how you can be a supportive wife and strong mother while your husband is working to bring in income. You mention keeping your faith, and that may very well be a good starting point. Faith, both in God and in your husband, is relatively easy while things are going well. Tough times call for us to exhibit that faith despite uncertainty. Keep reminding yourself that, in the final analysis, financial well-being, as well as all other aspects of our lives, is in God's hands, and that one of your most important tasks is to remain visibly appreciative of the blessings you have (children, family, health…) and for your husband's efforts.

It is important to think of yourself as a professional wife and mother. If you were a teacher or business executive during difficult times, you would still need to act calm and 'put on a good face.' That need is not less because you are in the home environment. You will find that as you exhibit a more positive outlook– even if it means putting on an act – it will eventually affect your mood as much as your family's. Remember that our feelings follow our actions as much as our actions follow our feelings.

Your husband and you should make sure that, without making your children feel insecure, you ensure that they are part of the team that lives within your means. Your job in particular is to make sure that they retain and exhibit respect for your husband. Their actions will be a reflection of what they see and feel from you. This might be a good opportunity to remind yourself and your children that 'wants' and 'needs' are two different categories. There may well be hidden blessings in the difficult times by focusing you on what truly matters, and the onus is on you to find the positive aspects and radiate that knowledge to your family.

As far as world events, we all need to straddle a line where we do what we can without being overwhelmed. You can give charity and vote wisely, but if might be a good idea to limit the time you spend listening to the news or bringing the outside world into your house. Without putting your head in the sand, you need to make your home a sanctuary.

We hope this gives you a starting place and pray that the coming months brings renewed prosperity to your family,

Rabbi Daniel and Susan Lapin

31.
Does The Torah Give Guidance Concerning Bankruptcy?

I attended a financial seminar at church and the question of bankruptcy came up. It was stated that the Bible does not allow or talk about bankruptcy.

Considering that God had a city of refuge for one who committed manslaughter, I would think He would have mercy for those who find themselves in an impossible financial situation.

Does the Torah give us any guidance concerning bankruptcy?

Chris P.

Dear Chris,

The answer to your question, "Does the Torah give us any guidance concerning bankruptcy?" is yes, although with a 'but.' The Bible gives us guidance for everything in our lives, including financial crises, but the word bankruptcy has a specific legal meaning in our times, and the Bible isn't bound by the legal system of any country or time.

Governments have struggled in many times and places with how to treat individuals who are unable to pay their debts. Solutions have ranged from debtor's prison as immortalized in Dickens' novels to erasing the debt and allowing the person to start afresh. The Torah's attitude is concerned with both the dignity of the individual in debt as well as with facilitating a society where people will interact economically. Debtor's prison negates the first concern while simply cancelling outstanding debts counters the second.

In general, if all other avenues of action have been exhausted, the Torah's path of redemption for someone who simply cannot meet his financial obligations would be somewhat similar to what used to be known as 'indentured servitude', in its most positive presentation. The individual would sell his services for a number of years (no more than six) to someone who in exchange, would pay off his obligations and take responsibility for mentoring and sustaining him for that period. It is a way for those who are owed money by the impoverished person to receive their payment and for the impoverished person to get breathing space and an opportunity to start over. The rules governing the interaction between the people involved are quite stringent, making sure that the arrangement is beneficial to both.

While this idea can't be applied outside of a completely Torah-run society, it does give insight into balancing the differing concerns that need to be taken into account.

Rabbi Daniel and Susan Lapin

32.
When a Financially Struggling Family Member Asks For a Loan

A few years ago, the Lord brought me out of financial disaster. I am applying the financial principles He's ministered to me and am prospering financially now (it took a few years to get here).

However, close members of my family are still struggling financially. When they ask me for a loan, I prayerfully consider my answer. When the answer is no, I often feel guilty because I feel obligated to help them because they are family, kind of like survivor's guilt I guess.

I try to always give them advice though. I know the Lord desires to prosper me financially even more than He already has. How do I become comfortable with being prosperous when close family members are still struggling?

Pam

Dear Pam,

How wonderful that you are seeing the Lord's blessings in your financial life. It sounds like you worked hard to make yourself worthy.

Guilt is an interesting emotion and one that can inspire or cripple. If we are doing something wrong and feel guilty about our actions, that feeling can spur us to repent and change our ways. Misplaced guilt leads people to hurt themselves and others. Many times when compassion and/or sadness would be appropriate feelings, guilt worms its way in instead, leading to unfortunate consequences.

For example, if one is blessed with a healthy child while one's friend miscarries, sensitivity and empathy are required. But guilt? No. Too many people who feel guilty about wealth end up supporting policies that end up keeping people in poverty rather than allowing them to flourish. Since you say that you prayerfully consider your relative's requests, we are guessing that you are recognizing that giving money before they have reconsidered their ways is counter-productive. If they are not open to your advice, giving that might be counter-productive as well.

If you are already tithing and charitable, it doesn't sound like guilt should be what you are feeling. Ideally, helping family should come before helping strangers, but the operative word is helping – not throwing money away. You might want to consider opening a savings account set aside for your family. If down the road they do behave more responsibly or if there is a child who shows promise and needs a hand, you would have that money set aside for them already. That would be a responsible and caring way to care for your family and you would be ready to help as soon as they are prepared to invest in their own future.

Rabbi Daniel and Susan Lapin

33.
Do I Owe My Alma Mater a Donation if They No Longer Represent My Values?

Sometime in the last year, I heard you discussing on the radio why conservative institutions over time turn liberal. I am in the midst of a personal dilemma.

My college has become a University over time because of large money donations. They are not a Catholic school as they were when I went to it. My husband and I give a donation every year to their Nursing Scholarships. This year they sent me a "Christmas" card which said Seasons Greetings. They also have had (politically liberal) speakers and have not offered any speakers on the other side of the political spectrum. My husband says my Conservative beliefs are too rigid. But I believe both sides of an argument should always be presented in a school setting.

I am considering not donating to my school because they have become too politically correct. When questioned they said only 35% of the school is Catholic and they must respect other belief systems. Can you help clarify my thoughts?

Elinor L.

Dear Elinor,

One of the things we love about the free market is that we can each donate money to the causes in which we believe. That is why we so strenuously object when we hear people speak about the government being charitable. Forcibly taking money from some people to give it away is not charity. Charity can only be a voluntary act done by an individual.

You should be commended for wanting to help others get the education you were fortunate to receive. However, your loyalty is to an idea, not to an institution. If the school still had the principles it did when you attended, then it would have priority over another school because of your personal connection. If it has changed, then you should certainly feel free to donate to a place that better reflects your values. As we frequently say, politics is nothing less than the practical application of our value system. As with any person of faith, you are fully entitled to apply your faith values to your political and economic choices.

The very fact that you think deeply about your charitable contributions suggests that you take your obligation seriously. We wouldn't call that being too rigid, but rather being discerning.

Rabbi Daniel and Susan Lapin

34.
Finding the Balance Between Ministry and Money

I'm a minister in the process of ordination for a Senior Pastoral position. I just purchased your book, Thou Shall Prosper and it is very insightful.

My question is, is it wrong to charge for the sermons that I preach and teach? I'm confused about this wealth process. Since I would actually be a public speaker is this one of the ways that I am to gain my wealth?

Stefon

Dear Stefon,

Congratulations on your upcoming ordination. We are assuming that you are not asking about charging for sermons in a venue where your job description includes speaking, but rather in cases where you can solicit extra speaking engagements that don't conflict with your obligations.

You should probably check with someone in your denomination as to what protocol is in your particular case, but we will give a general answer relating to discomfort about charging money for a service. This is a widespread problem.

A business owner, who sold items that catered to breast cancer survivors, told us how conflicted she was at charging the prices she needed to stay in business to people going through such difficult times. Indeed, the customers themselves occasionally implied that she should donate her products to them. That entirely misses the point. She is not running a charity, but a business. If she treats it like a charity, she will close her doors, doing neither herself nor others any favors. No one is compelled to buy from her and she is acting honorably and nobly by offering a warm atmosphere and needed services at a fair price.

Each of us has an obligation to be charitable with our time and money, but it is a personal obligation to be discharged how we see fit. That is very different from others assuming they have a right to our productivity.

You obviously need to function within the parameters of your denomination. Should your employment allow you to solicit speeches outside those parameters, we don't see any reason to feel guilty about offering a service for a fee as long as no one is compelled to employ you.

Wishing you success,

Rabbi Daniel and Susan Lapin

35.
Building Relationships While Taking Care of Yourself

I'm a single Christian. I have my own medical business.

All of my time is contributed into the business and reading the Bible or related materials. I haven't made any time for sports and any kind of entertainment or hobbies.

Just wondering from the Bible point of view, should I assign some time for those things?

D.L.

Dear D.L.,

If we were talking in person, we would ask you if you see a connection between your opening declaration and your closing question.

In our fast-paced society, many of us find it difficult to fit everything we need to do, ought to do, and want to do into the limited time we have.

Investing time into your business and into your relationship with God is important. So is staying physically fit and well-rounded. If you are asking the question, then our guess is that you are feeling stressed or out of kilter. This can happen when we separate parts of our life instead of integrating them. One benefit of sports and many hobbies is that they link us to other people. Instead of seeing your interest in the Bible as a solitary activity, we would urge you to find like-minded individuals with whom you can study, hike, play softball or do volunteer work. Don't view this time as slacking off. Building relationships with others and taking care of yourself will enhance your business abilities and your faith.

Expanding your horizons will also make clear to any future spouse that you have room in your life for a wife and family. Even more importantly, it will make it clear to you.

Rabbi Daniel and Susan Lapin

36.
Do I Tithe Before or After Taxes?

First, thank you for your teaching: It has been a great re-source for me, my bride and our 3 sons.

I heard you say that we should give 10% of our "after-tax" income. If we give based on after-tax income are we not first giving to the government and then secondly to God?

Many thanks for your time and I look forward to hearing from you.

Brad M.

Dear Brad,

We get asked this question frequently and, as always, we encourage people to speak to their own faith leaders. We can only tell you what ancient Jewish wisdom teaches.

We are not "giving to the government." The government is taking money from us. It is not a voluntary choice but a legal requirement. For that reason, it is more similar to getting a pay cut than to charity. If you had a 15% decrease in your salary, you wouldn't calculate your tithe on your past salary but on your new one. Realistically, our salaries are the money we receive after taxes have been taken from them.

This question relates to a larger mistake that we hear people making. Often people talk of the government giving charity.

That is not possible.

The government can allocate money and it can do so wisely or wastefully. If you give some of your money to a struggling neighbor, you are being compassionate and charitable. If the government gives some of your money to one of your struggling neighbors it is transferring funds and may or may not be practicing wise governance. As an entity rather than a human being, it is not being charitable. Charity is a uniquely human function.

Rabbi Daniel and Susan Lapin

37.
Expressing Ideas Fluently

Several months ago I remember reading a piece that you wrote in the Ziglar newsletter about secrets to improving business. One of the points was to read out loud to develop communication skills.

Would you be able to share some specific books that you find helpful to read out loud?

Joe

Dear Joe,

You may have the most wonderful skills and ideas, but they lose value if you aren't able to speak about them fluently. One way to make your presentation more fluent is to practice speaking. A first step on that path can be to read other people's words aloud.

We suggest that you start by reading famous speeches rather than a book. We personally enjoy the speeches of Winston Churchill, but Abraham Lincoln's *Gettysburg address* and Martin Luther King's *I Have a Dream speech* are also excellent. Try a variety of different styles and see how you can adapt your language to speak more forcefully. Take note of the language used. To speak successfully you may need to move out of your comfort zone and practice expanding your vocabulary or varying your intonation.

For variety, find a small child and read pre-school books to him. Changing your voice, inflection and speed as you become the different characters in the book is a wonderful way to get comfortable with a wider range of vocalization. Little kids are wonderful critics – they won't ask you to read the book again if you are boring. Once you have read the book a dozen or so times, try to tell it, by heart, to a different child, unfamiliar with the plot. It doesn't matter if you change some words, you will know if you can keep your young friend's attention.

One way to succeed in business is to make sure you have something of value to add to a company. However, you also need to be able to let others know of your assets and this is most often done through effective speaking.

Keep practicing,

Rabbi Daniel and Susan Lapin

38.
What Does the Torah Say About Gambling?

What does the Torah say about gambling?

Herlinda C.

Herlinda,

Let's starts by defining the term 'gambling.' As we are going to discuss it in this answer, gambling is an activity of chance which one engages in hoping to win money. The gambler provides no service or product of any value to any other human being in exchange for his winnings. Each participant in the activity is there mainly because he hopes that he can win while the others lose.

For this reason, the Torah looks down upon the professional gambler – meaning one who derives his income through gambling. Why? Because the Torah encourages activities in which all participants are winners. If we come into your furniture store and purchase a couch, everyone is happy. We have a couch and you have money. If you mow our lawn in exchange for an agreed upon fee, we both are happy. The time and effort saved is worth the money in our eyes and you are happy with your payment. Ideally, all business transactions should be like this.

However, if a group plays poker and each person is playing

in order to win money, then at the end of the evening one person is happy and the rest of the group are discontented. Had they known in advance that they would lose, they would not have played. If you spend an evening putting money into a slot machine and don't win, you are left with an empty and disgusted feeling. If you do win, it is random; and the Torah frowns on directing our lives in a random fashion.

We each have innate skills that we are to use in this world. Our goal is not to coast through this world focused on ourselves but to connect with others and make the world a better place. The soul-destroying activity of gambling violates this rule.

Rabbi Daniel and Susan Lapin

39.
Do I Need to Tell My Wife about Money I Inherited?

I have not told my wife about some money I received. My intent was to invest it in a business venture and surprise everyone with my ability to make big things happen. Though we have a great relationship for 20+ years and care very much for each other, we greatly differ in our approach to business. I have always worked and loved my wife, and our children are well educated, college wise. Still, I have suffered from some failure in being a good provider and see an opportunity to start my own business. Am I wrong in what I've done?

Warren

Dear Warren,

Your email raises a number of important issues, among them trust in marriage and attitudes towards business. We believe that your intentions are good, but we all know what road is paved with good intentions.

You absolutely cannot start a business without understanding that there is no guarantee of being able to, "surprise everyone with my ability to make big things happen." Not only is there a chance for failure, but you will need to invest a great deal of your energy and time in order to make a success. Doing that while keeping it a secret from you wife will be impossible. You are setting up the conditions for failure.

We would strongly advise you and your wife to find a money/ business management course that you can take together. You need to try and understand your wife's attitude to money as well as your own, and to honestly ask whether there is truth in at least some of what she would say. In answering her questions and reservations you may find that you build the strong foundation needed for accomplishing your goals.

You are missing an opportunity to build both a stronger marriage and a stronger business. You have a substantially greater chance of success if the two of you believe in the venture and support each other. You will hit tough times in any business and you will need your wife's support rather than adding guilt and recriminations to the difficult times.

Congratulations on coming into some money. Working in an honest and realistic way with your wife and with business mentors will help you to use it well.

Rabbi Daniel and Susan Lapin

40.
A Widow Loses Her Spouse and Gains a Huge Responsibility

I've been widowed now a year and 5 months. I'm 59 years old, and instantly became responsible for running my late husband's business. I just recently ordered Thou Shall Prosper.

With all this new responsibility...it got a little overwhelming. I called on the mercy of God, and am trusting like I have never trusted before. A new walk of faith for me. The question I have for you is, well...I have to find purpose in my life. I seem to have such a sense of lack. My duty as a wife gave me a sense of purpose. I need advice on this, because I truly need to find myself again. I don't know where or how to begin again. I feel like I'm doing everything because I have to be responsible.

Help me out if you can. I really am looking forward to your response.

Sonya K.

Dear Sonya,

We want to offer both our condolences and our admiration. Only a little over a year ago, you lost your life partner as well as acquired a business overnight.

The emotional adjustment is huge. You are just now getting

past the point of all those "firsts" – first Thanksgiving, first birthday without your husband, etc. In addition to that, you accepted the responsibility of running your husband's business. Please don't underestimate the strength, courage and conviction you have displayed or the shock waves your system is still absorbing.

You have turned to God, which is, of course, vitally important. We would suggest that you also work on building a network of human support. While you need to be careful that you not get involved with people who will prey on your vulnerabilities, we all need human relationships. As you are strengthened by others, you will naturally find that you have much to offer them, which will give you a re-directed purpose.

You found meaning in your role as a wife, and you may find that carrying on your husband's work becomes an extension of that. Providing employment for some and a valuable service or product for others is a worthy purpose. One emotionally intense year as a businesswoman is too short a time for you to know if you can get satisfaction from this venue.

Perhaps, after obtaining wise and experienced advice and counsel, you may turn much of the business operation over to someone else. Another, unexpected avenue may open. Perhaps you will be drawn to mentoring young wives who don't have a role model. You might find fulfillment in one of the thousands of opportunities for giving that surround us.

Please be patient and gentle with yourself. You enjoyed the blessing of a good marriage, which eludes so many, and we pray that there are still many blessings waiting for you.

Rabbi Daniel and Susan Lapin

41.
Can I Help My Son Pick
the Right Career?

How can I help my 19 year old son pick what is right for him as career training? I am so perplexed at his ideas that to me do not seem to match him at all. I believe he should pick something within his personality and natural talents, but what do you think?
Thank you!

Vicky R.

Dear Vicky,

We hope you don't find our response too abrupt and we certainly don't want to sound unfeeling, but the answer to your initial question is – you can't! At nineteen, your son needs to make some choices of his own and to live with the consequences of those choices.

You may be correct in thinking he is opting for career choices for which he isn't suited, but you might also be completely wrong. Many highly successful adults pursued career paths that astound all who knew them when they were younger. We have one friend who struggled with math through her school years and was convinced she was 'no good with numbers.' In college, she discovered that while she truly doesn't like arithmetic, she actually loves other aspects of mathematics and she now earns her living quite happily in a mathematical field.

Whether or not you are assessing your son accurately, he is old enough to be given the opportunity to stretch his own wings. However, there is an addendum to our comments. He is also old enough to be transitioning to becoming responsible for himself. While, we feel that you should give him emotional support for his choices, and of course, lots of love, you have every right and even the duty to make clear exactly what the limitations are on your financial support. Each family will be different, but you can certainly let him know how much, if any, of his studies you can assist with, which of his needs you expect him to take care of himself, and what the limits are for how long you will help him.

The bottom line is that it is time for mutual respect. You must respect his ability to direct his own way in life. He needs to respect and appreciate what you have done for him throughout his childhood and to recognize that adult responsibilities accompany making adult decisions. If your relationship is built on love, this transition to adulthood can be an exciting time for both of you.

Wishing you well,

Rabbi Daniel and Susan Lapin

42.
Earning Money Can Be Among Life's Most Virtuous Activities

(Our) pastor made a comment that, "If you made $20,000 per month you are probably selling drugs or something else illegal."

He was talking about people getting into late night infomercial deals, but I have noticed, that he just doesn't think that God blesses abundantly.

I would greatly appreciate your input since my husband has had some months where he brought home $25,000. And he hasn't done anything illegal. He just works really hard and doesn't apologize for being successful.

Jennifer L.

Dear Jennifer,

We spend a great deal of time helping people see that earning money can be among life's most virtuous activities.

Unfortunately, not only some pastors but also many politicians and citizens do not have an understanding of ethical capitalism. For example, calling money earned through investments "unearned income" shows a lack of comprehension of what investment means. Investing means taking a risk and not using money one has for another purpose. When the investment pays off, and often it does not, it is foolish to act as if the investor simply found money while walking down the road. Similarly, terms like "giving back to society" imply that while working and earning money, one is a taker. That couldn't be further from the truth.

It sounds like you and your husband are a hard-working couple who accept the insecurity of not having a fixed income but instead have large returns when your hard work succeeds. You should certainly either look for a church that appreciates people like you. You could also try to educate the pastor. May we suggest giving him some of our financial resources?

Wishing you much continued success,

Rabbi Daniel and Susan Lapin

43.
Working Hard, but Staying at the Same Level - What's Wrong?

I run my delivery business for 10 years. My drivers and I are always sharp and effective in doing deliveries. I put all my time and efforts into this business. I have tried different marketing tools, joined different networking groups. Unfortunately, I am stuck at the same level I was 3 years ago. Even my best clients give me less and less business.

What am I doing I do wrong?

Alex S.

Dear Alex,

We are sorry that you are having such a tough time. Clearly, we can't comment about your particular case based on a short question from you, but we hope we can provide a few 'food for thought' concepts.

The first thing to realize is that with the economy the way it has been for the past few years, keeping the same level of business is not a small thing. While it may not be bringing in as much income as you like, many businesses are contracting or not managing to survive at all. Your clients may not be growing themselves, the consequences of which are affecting you. Maintaining your business is a sign that you are doing quite a lot correctly.

However, you understandably want to grow. Here are a few things to consider.

1)   It is great that you have tried networking and marketing. The fact that they have not yielded results doesn't mean that you should drop those efforts. If there is anyone who is business savvy who could review those efforts with you, it might be helpful. Perhaps there are better ways to try or sometimes, campaigns need more time to work than we would like them to take. One mistake many business people make is not realizing how much of marketing builds upon name recognition and how long that takes to build.

2)   With gas prices going up, we assume that your costs are going up as well, and traditional delivery methods are being hard hit. Have you considered looking at your customer's needs and working backwards to see if there is another service you could offer that would align with what you are already doing while providing more value?

3)   Do you get regular feedback from your customers? Do you stay in touch even between business transactions? Do you track what the competition is doing? Information is priceless.

The economy right now is a difficult one. It makes it hard for a business to succeed and increasingly seeks to punish those that do succeed (making a vicious cycle). This is one of those periods where determination, resourcefulness and creativity are especially valuable.

Rabbi Daniel and Susan Lapin

44.
I No Longer Love What I Do

I am a candlemaker. I have been doing this for almost 16 years.

I have a retail storefront and wholesale. I have also franchised a couple of times. I am quite blessed to do what I love for a living. Lately, however, it seems that I work for everyone else; the wax company, the fragrance companies, the wick company. It has really taken the drive I used to have from me.

How do I change my attitude?

Marsha M.

Dear Marsha,

It sounds as if you have been blessed in both doing what you love and loving what you do for many years. You don't describe why it now seems that you work for everyone else. Are you not producing the profit that would persuade you that you are indeed working effectively? Remember that profit is a vital part of any business. It comes ahead even of loving what you do.

Assuming that you are profitable, remember that businesses, like personal relationships, are always fluid. Both external and internal factors change.

Before you can change your attitude, you have to decide what your goal is. All work has some negative elements. If the negative elements are consistently outweighing the positive ones, you may need a restructuring rather than an attitude change.

Perhaps you need to bring in someone to handle more of the vendor/franchisee relationships leaving you more time to design and make candles. Of course, this step has the potential to be wonderful if done correctly with the right person, or a nightmare if handled incorrectly and/or with the wrong person. That makes it a huge and scary step to explore.

Not knowing your business, we may be on the wrong track. While flitting from one thing to another isn't productive, when you have been in the same business for many years, you might re-ignite a passion by thinking outside the box and exploring different options. Try soliciting ideas and advice from craftsmen and business owners you admire. Talk to a mentor.

While we believe strongly in generating a positive mind-set and attitude, sometimes very real and tangible changes need to take place.

Wishing you good fortune and happiness in your endeavors,

Rabbi Daniel and Susan Lapin

45.
What is God's Ideal
Economic System?

Would the Old Testament government established by God (with respect to the economic model/system) be considered conservative/capitalistic or socialistic/communal?

Thank you for your time!

Chris L

Dear Chris,

You are asking us a question along the line of, "Was yesterday the first time you hit your wife? Answer yes or no."

None of the economic systems we think of today, such as capitalism or socialism, represent God's vision for an economic system. We personally say that we can't define ourselves as conservatives or liberals in a general sense. We can only look at the ideologies and policies of those views as they are expressed today and judge which come closest to the Torah way. In a different time or place, we might find ourselves supporting the opposite trend.

Communism and socialism are clearly not the Torah way, but neither is unbridled capitalism. We like to use the term "ethical capitalism," a term we created. This is our attempt to come closer to the Torah view. However, an economic system is only part of an entire range of life systems, and all the parts need to match to bring us closer to implementing God's plan for us on earth.

We hope this helps.

Rabbi Daniel and Susan Lapin

46.
Why is Retirement
Such a Bad Thing?

Could you re-explain to a 73 year old man the bad aspect of retirement? Please explain again the Jewish meaning of it.

I have been retired for over ten years.

Sherman F.

Dear Sherman,

You are referring to my claim that since there is no word in Hebrew for retirement the concept should not exist. While my wife and I rarely disagree, I'm afraid you might be giving her an "I told you so" moment. When I rail against retirement in speeches, she worries how the 93-year-old man in the audience is hearing my words. Then, you are still young, so even she would agree that you have no call to be retired.

Perhaps I can clear things up if I explain that I don't think that one has to stay in the same job for a lifetime. What I do mean is that at no point should anyone think that they no longer need to do things for others, but can spend time only seeking their own enjoyment.

For men in particular, I think that evaluating whether you are truly helping others is best judged by whether people are willing to pay you for your efforts. While there is certainly a place for volunteer work, rather than doing only that, I would encourage working for payment even if you then choose to donate much of your salary.

I hope this helps clear things up.

Rabbi Daniel and Susan Lapin

47.
My Friend Cheated Me!

A few years ago I was cheated by a man who said he loved God and attended church almost daily. He was also a very good friend and I trusted him completely. I invested a big chunk of my savings in his company which he told me was going public. He filed bankruptcy and I had no recourse at all. How do I handle this? I am single and have to work very hard to make ends meet. I appreciate your consideration.

Amy

Dear Amy,

How sad that you lost so much of your savings. We're sure you wish you'd asked a professional for financial advice before putting so many of your eggs in one basket. We assume you aren't asking us for legal advice but rather want help dealing with bad feelings towards your friend and perhaps feelings of despair for yourself.

While it is hard for us to comment without knowing more details, and perhaps we are misreading your question, your friend may very well be an upright, honorable man whose business plans failed. As crushing as it is to have a business failure, especially when you lose other people's money, it doesn't necessarily reflect on character. If this is the case, you might feel cruelly disappointed but not betrayed. If there was a deliberate swindle, or if poor choices (like vacationing rather than working hard) were present, then the story is different, of course.

In terms of your own financial situation right now, we can very much sympathize. When you are working hard to make ends meet, losing a savings cushion can be devastating. Like so much else in life, while you might look to see if you can improve your income stream, what you have even more control over is improving your attitude. We strongly advise you to find some way of giving to those who have less than you, be it less money, less health, less faith, less family...Being a giver allows us to focus on what we have rather than what we don't have and enlarges our spirit. It encourages us to look forward rather than backward.

We hope you find a local mentor and group of friends to help you through this difficult time,

Rabbi Daniel and Susan Lapin

48.
Expanding Relationships to Increase Opportunities

Shalom: My husband and I are both I.T. Engineers. He has more certifications than I, but right now I am working and he is not. He has been running another business for now, but customers most often cannot afford his services, no matter how he lowers costs for them.

He feels embarrassed before our children, although we greatly admire him. He brings us together for daily Torah story and prayer. He encourages us that times will get better. I believe character over currency. Please tell me what else can we do for him?

Tirtzah

Dear Tirtzah,

Our hearts go out to you. When someone we love is suffering, we wish for the 'magic bullet' or 'miracle statement' with which we can make everything better. Unfortunately, they don't exist. Life has challenges that we can't make go away. It sounds to us as if your family is doing so much right. Maintaining respect for your husband, daily Torah study and trying to find new revenue streams are all important. It speaks well to your husband's character that he is not happy with the status quo. He wants to support his family and be an economically productive member of society.

If there is one piece of advice we might respectfully offer, it is that you encourage your husband to expand his relationships outside of the immediate family. Having other Godly men with whom to share his troubles would give him emotional support that he cannot accept from you. Enlarging his circle of friends will also put him in a better position to hear of job opportunities and to spur creative thinking as to how his talents can be employed.

Hoping to hear positive news soon,

Rabbi Daniel and Susan Lapin

49.
Should I Give Money to Beggars?

*In Thought Tools from January 8, 2009, you refer to Deuter-
onomy 22:4 and say, "From this verse, ancient Jewish wisdom teaches that God wants us to help only those who are
doing everything possible to help themselves."*

*I have always felt it morally wrong to give a beggar on the
street any money for the reason stated above. I always treat
them with respect and say "No thank you" then wish them
a pleasant day. Am I acting in a moral fashion? I ask because you begin this installment with the story of the man
giving the beggar a dollar everyday and it made me question
whether or not I am acting in a moral fashion or not.*

I would love your thoughts here,

Bryan Y.

Dear Bryan,

In that Thought Tool from early 2009, we pointed out how
the words in Deuteronomy 22:4 say that you should help
your brother right his donkey if it falls. It doesn't say that you
should right his donkey independent from any of his actions.

In many real-life situations, we need to do things that are a
combination of right and wrong. It is rare to find an action
that is only good, with no negative consequences or aspects
at all. For example, if I go to visit a friend in the hospital – a

loving action – it may mean I miss dinner with my children or leave work a little early—hurting my family ties or ignoring my financial needs.

There are two aspects to giving money to a beggar. The first is helping him. We all know that in many cases all we are helping a street person to do is buy drugs or alcohol, or allowing a severely mentally ill person to stay on the streets for a little longer. However, there is a second side to giving money as well. We are refining our own character by not allowing ourselves to ignore a suffering person.

When someone would approach me when my children were very young and with me, I would usually give because I wanted my children to learn the lesson of charity and they were too young to understand nuances. When I am by myself, I rarely give, because I think I may simply be wasting money, which is not a neutral action, but a wrong one. I do try to make a point to give the money I could have given to the person on the street to one of the many worthwhile and successful charities that actually help those who truly can be helped.

Rabbi Daniel and Susan Lapin

50.
I Want to Help Others!

I need help so badly, not for myself, but for helping others! Me and my congregation would like to open a secondhand shop but we do not have enough money for the rent. What do you suggest we do in this case? How can we help others if we do not have the means for it?

Yehudit B.

Dear Yehudit,

We appreciate the opportunity to expand on the concept of helping others. One of the points we stress in our teachings, is that making money in an honest and moral way is good in and of itself. Giving to charity is then an additional good which money allows one to do.

When it comes to giving, it is important not to be caught up in the thinking, "If I earned more, I could give charity," or "When I have enough money, I will give charity." One of the reasons that Scripture speaks of giving as a percentage, a tenth, is because no matter how much or little you have, you can isolate a tenth of that amount. It is terribly damaging for anyone not to see himself or herself as a giver, but only as a taker. We all must give charity.

Our suggestion would be that you change your thinking from what you can do when you have the funds to what you can do now. A second-hand shop is wonderful, but you need to start with something that is within your means and then work up to more. Maybe you can run a 'clothing swap' regularly where people get together and trade items. If a few people supply some drinks and cakes it can be a lovely social opportunity. Each participant can also pay a very low amount, maybe $5.00 and that money can be put aside to support a second-hand store down the road.

There is a fantastic concept in the Jewish community, known as a gemach. That word is actually an acronym for the Hebrew phrase "gemilut chassadim" or "giving kindness." These gemachs are run by both individuals and organizations. A person might let it be known that they have some item such as baby supplies, which they will lend out to anyone who needs. Other people, for example, a family whose children have outgrown a highchair, will add to that person's supply. This type of gemach is usually run from a spare room or a family's basement. A family with young children that cannot afford new things, or even grandparents with visiting grandchildren will borrow these items. Usually, they contribute a minimal sum to replenish the supply and keep the gemach going. There are gemachs for wedding dresses, medical supplies and just about anything else one can imagine people needing. It is a way for neighbors to help each other.

You and your congregation need to focus on what you can do now. Don't allow wanting to accomplish something big stop you from starting with what is possible today. In addition, remember that offering time is as important as offering money. Providing baby-sitting, inviting someone for a meal, and driving someone to a medical appointment are all ways in which we can give to others.

Wishing you success,

Rabbi Daniel and Susan Lapin

51.
Why Are Some People Seemingly Blessed More Than Others?

I need an answer to this puzzling question. Not everyone in the Bible was blessed in the same measure. Today's Ministers are teaching that all people of the earth should obtain the great blessing of wealth.

Thanks,

Evelyn P.

Dear Evelyn,

We'd like to approach your question in two ways. The majority of people in many countries today, even those who are considered poor by their governments, live in luxury compared to many people in other countries or even to wealthy people in the past. If you can be considered poor while having food on the table, air-conditioning and TV, you have to agree that the definition of poor is very fluid. That is a very different level of poverty than starving in the street.

God treats us both as individuals and as members of our society. The millions that starved in Russia or China in the last century were victims not of God or nature, but of their governments. When a society as a whole follows the path of what we might call Judeo-Christian values, then life in that society, even for those who are comparatively not well off, is pretty good.

At the same time, we do believe that God allocates a certain amount of wealth to each individual. Our task is to access the storehouse that He has set aside for us. While some individuals might have the potential for relatively little and some for massive amounts, most of us can probably assume that we can get more than we are currently getting. In the same way that we humans use only a small part of our brain capacity and waste vast quantities of time, we most likely don't maximize our earning potential either. If ten people are blessed with their maximum allocation, they will each get different amounts, but in almost all cases, they will be doing well indeed.

We need to keep one eye on our society and one eye on ourselves. When both the people among whom we live, and each of us individually, follow basic Biblical rules, life—for just about everybody— can be blessed indeed.

Wishing you well,

Rabbi Daniel and Susan Lapin

Questions & Answers
About Faith

52.
Do Jews Believe in an Afterlife?

Do Jewish people believe in life after death? Since I was a little girl I have been terrified of death. As I have gotten older, the hope of heaven seems more and more like a scam. Did God really create us to share eternity with Him, or are our own egos and pride unable to accept oblivion? My faith in any God seems tied up in this paradox. So many religions have so many answers that make no sense to me.

Thank you,

Kathleen R.

Dear Kathleen,

The Torah, Judaism's constitution, absolutely believes in an existence after death while at the same time very much focusing on our existence in this world. The important part of the soul remaining 'alive' even after our bodies stop functioning is that we will be judged on the actions that our souls and bodies took when they were coupled. We will need to account for both the good and the bad that we did in this world. Our lives in the 'world to come' will be based on that accounting. Judaism also declares that the Messiah will bring about a resurrection of the dead.

Our understanding of both these ideas is as limited as our comprehension of what lies beyond the furthest reaches of the furthest galaxy, and for the same reason: God created us

119

with limited ability to comprehend that which He chooses to keep from us.

We observe that so much of the things that matter most to us in life are spiritual in nature. We also know that while material things perish, corrode or decay, spiritual things like songs, sentiments and souls endure forever. We enter that eternal world once our beings are confined only to the spiritual.

Other than accepting these ideas, very little time is given to picturing the details. It is beyond our comprehension. Instead, Judaism focuses on how we should live our lives while our bodies and souls are together. An awareness of a 'world to come' reminds us that our actions matter for eternity and that we must take advantage of being alive in order to make wise decisions. Our important choices each day revolve around doing the right thing while we are alive, not ignoring the important things in this life while focusing on the next one.

Hope this helps,

Rabbi Daniel and Susan Lapin

53.
My Research Doesn't Match
What You Say

*I watched you and Susan on TCT talk about Yom Kippur
and you said the word afflict is the Hebrew word ve-eenitem
and it also means to answer. Your teaching is wonderful but
when I look in Strong's Concordance the Hebrew word used
in Numbers and Leviticus is 6031, anah (sorry I can't punc-
tuate or write Hebrew).*

Shalom, Shalom,

Rich M.

Dear Rich,

We get quite a few 'Ask the Rabbi' questions letting us know
that Strong's Concordance doesn't show what we are teaching. What can we say? While you can make a dictionary or
concordance of Biblical words, that is a pragmatic, material-
istic treatment of the material. It treats Hebrew as it would
treat any other language.

The Bible and the Hebrew words in it function on that level
but they also have deep spiritual significance. In each of our
Genesis Journeys audio CDs and in our book *Buried Treasure*, we try to show how Hebrew is God's language and it
acts completely differently from any other language. The

ideas that words that share root letters share meaning, that many important words need to be read forward and backwards, and that the numerical value of the letters is important are only three insights that the Concordance doesn't reveal. These treasures and many more have been passed down through the generations since Moses on Sinai and it is what we refer to as ancient Jewish wisdom.

You might think of Strong's Concordance as one ingredient in your Bible study, but it isn't the whole recipe.

Keep studying,

Rabbi Daniel and Susan Lapin

54.
Is Judaism Specifically a Religion for the Jews?

Is Judaism specifically a religion for the Jews, or was it intended to be the religion of the world?

James Y.

Dear James,

You are asking a question that highlights one of the major differences between Judaism and many other religions. Although Judaism welcomes sincere converts, it does not seek them out. It stresses that all human beings have the ability to relate to God and attain a place in Heaven.

Just as priests and Levites have unique responsibilities within the Jewish people, and as such can rise higher spiritually—and sink lower—than the majority of Jews can, we believe that Jews occupy that same niche in regards to the rest of the world. Historically, this explains the tremendous and disproportionate number of both positive and negative influences that Jews have brought to the world. When we fulfill our mission, both the world and we are blessed. When we fail in our mission, we harm both the world and ourselves.

The Torah and ancient Jewish wisdom contain valuable information for everyone, not just for Jews. Just as an applied mathematics or physics textbook contains technical information relevant mostly for mathematicians and physicists, each one also reveals useful information on how the world REALLY works that is helpful to all. Similarly, while the Torah has rules intended only for Jews as well as ones intended for all mankind, it also conveys vital information on how the world REALLY works that is helpful to all of us in achieving our Divine destiny and our mission.

May you fulfill your own mission,

Rabbi Daniel and Susan Lapin

55.
Observing the Sabbath and Keeping It Holy

I am aware that there have been various questions already asked regarding observing the Sabbath and keeping it Holy, but my problem is the company I work for has offered me a promotion but it entails me studying on a Saturday morning. What is your stance on studying secular studies on the Sabbath?

Adele

Dear Adele,

Your question, in itself, shows a great degree of sensitivity to the Sabbath. Many people mistakenly think that the Sabbath in religious Jewish homes consists of a list of things that are forbidden. Indeed, there are many things we do not do on Shabbat including writing, cooking and handling money. Rather than being oppressive, these restrictions allow Shabbat to blossom and be the precious gift that God intended it to be. Shabbat is an invigorating and refreshing change from the other six days of the week.

For this reason, a bigger picture is needed. One can decide not to write but mentally obsess on what needs to be communicated when Shabbat is over; refrain from cooking but worry about meal planning for the coming week; not handle money but be preoccupied thinking about business. These mental activities will prevent you from getting the full benefit of Shabbat.

Each person and situation is unique and so we hesitate to answer your question with a 'yes' or 'no'. In the final analysis, this is a decision you must make for yourself (possibly with the help of a religious leader who knows you). With the sensitivity you are exhibiting, we think that you cherish the Sabbath and will hesitate to do anything that might intrude on its specialness.

Wishing you well,

Rabbi Daniel and Susan Lapin

56.
Did the Patriarchs and Matriarchs Know the Torah?

I read and discussed with a couple of my friends regarding your Thought Tool - Don't Ask – Do Tell. You talked about the relevance of the bracelet and gold ring Rebekah received to the 10 Commandments.

The part that I was confused about was, how would this be relevant at this point in time? Rebekah wouldn't have known about the 10 Commandments yet. Moses was not born yet and God had not given the 10 Commandments to him until Exodus 20.

Maybe I am missing something but I had a hard time seeing the relevance that you presented in the article. I appreciate your time.

Best Regards,

Anonymous

Dear Anonymous,

We received many emails about this and appreciate that you and others told us that our writing presumed background information. Ancient Jewish wisdom tells us that God created the world using the Torah as His blueprint. If it only came into being at Mt. Sinai, how could that be? It is a way of saying that the Torah is a timeless description of universal reality. Only our limited understanding has us seeing parts of it as obscure and irrelevant.

Recently, signs went up in a park near our house stating that plants may not be harvested. Someone reading those signs might think what a good idea it is to make that prohibition known. Surely before the signs were posted, the park's foliage was regularly decimated. Nothing could be further from the truth. Until recently, the population shared a common civic understanding not to uproot the park's plants. The signs were not needed until many residents didn't share that civic understanding.

The patriarchs and matriarchs intuitively understood the Torah, including the foundational description of how people and societies thrive. They did not need to be presented with the Ten Commandments; they had an instinctive comprehension of them. Have you ever known exactly what your spouse was going to say before she said it? These great forebears of ours were so in tune with God and His creation that they could have recited the Ten Commandments centuries before they were shared with the nation of Israel and through them, all humanity.

We hope that this helps to explain the Thought Tool,

Rabbi Daniel and Susan Lapin

57.
Aren't There Many Rules in the Bible That Don't Make Sense?

Many people make the claim that the laws regarding homo-
sexuality in the book of Leviticus can be ignored because Le-
viticus has other laws that do not make sense, like a prohibi-
tion on wearing clothes woven of two kinds of material or
planting a field with two kinds of seed. (Lev. 19: 19) I can see
that other laws make good sense, but why these particular
laws on clothing and planting?

David J.

Dear David,

We had not heard the claim you describe but can understand
why it might sound disturbing. Let's talk for a minute, about
some laws in Leviticus 'not making sense.' You can imagine some smart 19th century folks believing that the notion
of time and space being part of the same continuum and
relative to one another doesn't make sense. Of course, once
Minkowski and Einstein based modern physics upon that
notion, it began to make a lot of sense.

Similarly, someone knowing nothing about radiation might
assume that warnings about invisible but dangerous rays em-
anating from rock-like chunks of uranium make no sense.

Many people think it makes no sense when we explain how

humans were created with certain built-in characteristics. For instance, most of us don't do well when our lifestyle undergoes sudden and dramatic change. We thrive when necessary change is slow and incremental. Someone with no understanding of human physiology might think it makes no sense, but it makes a lot of sense.

We also thrive better in a world of difference and contrast than in a world of constant uniformity. For instance, our bodies suffer under conditions of 24-hour light or 24-hour darkness. We need both light and darkness. We thrill to the reality of sexual difference and posterity is assured by that difference. It is partially the existence of death that imparts to life its almost unbearably ecstatic moments.

Much of the Torah is devoted to helping prevent the erosion of difference in our perception of reality. There are many laws that invoke separation - of dairy and meat foods, of men and women, of wool and linen and not planting together certain kinds of seeds. We follow them to this very day, because God told us to, but they also serve the purpose of helping to maintain a spirit of separation in our souls and add to the fullness of our life experience.

Part of the problem with homosexuality is that over the long term, and with many involved, it erodes vital distinctions between men and women and ultimately collapses the attraction between them. We are so pleased you wrote on this important and widely misunderstood topic.

Rabbi Daniel and Susan Lapin

58.
Life Isn't Fair

*Why are we all made so uneven? Some are born into afflu-
ence and some into poverty. Some are born into health some
into misery. Some are born in America, with all its advan-
tages, some into primitive tribes.*

*Well you get the idea. Some people believe this unevenness
can be blamed on some evil thing the infant does. This doesn't
seem right to me. Some believe this can be blamed on what
some ancestor did. This doesn't seem right either. How can
all this be the result of a benevolent and omnipotent Creator?*

William D.

Dear William,

Your questions plagues most thinking people at one point or
another as they mature and recognize that, "Life isn't fair." It
is not a new question, yet each era brings its own challenges,
and one of the trials of our particular time is the difficulty
we have in acknowledging that we cannot understand God's
ways. Humility comes hard to us.

It is difficult for our human minds to reconcile, "Life isn't fair,"
with the idea of a benevolent and omnipotent Creator. That is
one of the challenges of faith. From our limited perspective,
life certainly isn't fair, but there actually isn't a word for 'fair'
in Hebrew, which implies that the concept doesn't exist. The
word 'just' however, can be frequently found – TSeDeK. God
is a God of justice and one of our tasks is to work on bringing

justice to His world.

According to ancient Jewish wisdom, babies are born with pure souls and we can only sin once we are capable of making choices. A baby cannot, by definition, sin. Nonetheless, the reality is that some babies are born ill or into awful families or situations. It needs to be enough for us that God understands the reasons for this even when we do not.

One analogy related in Jewish tradition is the way that the underside of a needlepoint tapestry looks. It is a messy mixture of colored threads with no discernible pattern. Yet, when you turn the needlepoint over, a beautiful picture emerges. Our perspective comes from the vantage of the underside. God sees the magnificent final picture.

We are not enormous fans of John Rawls, a famous American political philosopher, but he did come up with an interesting idea: Suppose a genie came to you twenty four hours before you were born and offered you the opportunity to design the political, cultural, and economic system into which you would be born. The only snag is that you have no idea whether you'll be born to a rich family or a poor one, or whether you'll be born male or female, black or white, super smart or below average. Now you would want to choose some system that would give the best shot to the most people for the longest time.

What is helpful about this little thought experiment is the context of your question—how lucky to be born in America rather than to a primitive tribe in New Guinea. However, God's point is that nobody, yes, nobody needed to be born to primitive tribes or into repressive and horrible regimes. He gave us a blueprint for the best societal living called the Bible. Those countries that came closest to following it developed medicine, science, extended life, travel and exploration, and affluence. As some of those cultures traveled the world promoting a Biblical vision, the standard of living in many countries rose. However, so called 'colonization' became politically demonized, and so many countries were plunged back into barbarism. Many other countries have yet to see the light and make it out.

Ample evidence already exists to make the case that what separates successful countries from dismal failures is not geography, race, or weather. It is nothing but culture—another word for the transcendent idea people gain for their existence from whomever they worship.

God is saying, "Look, I have given you proof and proof again that the Bible guides everyone to a better life. It is horrible that anyone has to be born into a cruel tribal life but it doesn't have to be that way. I just need you all, Jews and Christians, to show the way to the light."

Rabbi Daniel and Susan Lapin

59.
Does God Have a Plan for My Life?

I recently celebrated my 32nd birthday. Every year at this time, I feel as though I have wandered aimlessly through the wilderness with no particular target. Does God have a plan for my life, or am I supposed to plan my own path and ask Him to bless it?

Christopher J.

Christopher,

Your letter is a well-written variation of a question that we frequently get. We hope it doesn't frustrate you too much if we say that our answer to your question is "both." We do believe that God places potential for certain things in each of us and His desire is for us to maximize that potential. A popular Jewish story tells of a rabbi named Zushya who lived in the 1700's. On his deathbed, his students saw him crying and tried to comfort him by assuring him that he had nothing to fear from a Heavenly court as he was as wise as Moses. He answered, "God isn't going to ask me why I wasn't Moses; He is going to ask me why I wasn't Zushya."

In other words, each of us is uniquely created. The problem, as you have discovered, is that we don't get an instruction manual taped to our umbilical cord. One of the exciting parts of life's journey is discovering our highest calling. Even if there are diversions on our path to the best, we should always ask God's blessing on what we do, and examine our actions to make sure that they are in accord with His rules. We can do greater things by committing all our resources to a second-ary path rather than halfheartedly doing something closer to our unique mission. In this world, we can only do our best at whatever we do.

By the age of 32, you should be immersed in some way to serve your fellow man. You should also be living as an adult in your personal life, either married and raising a family or well on your way to that. It would be a mistake to keep on getting degree after degree or to spend most of your time on extraneous activities because you haven't "found yourself." It is always easier to find yourself and your path while you are active and busy with worthwhile pursuits.

Once you are prospering (both financially and personally), if you still feel emptiness within you, then by all means, explore various paths and different fields of endeavor in your spare time.

We wish you a fulfilling year,

Rabbi Daniel and Susan Lapin

60.
Does God Love Men
More Than Women?

*I know this will sound silly, but it comes from the heart of a
wounded child. Does God love men more than women?*

Pamela P.

Dear Pamela,

Your question doesn't sound silly at all. Our first instinct,
however, was silly – simply to answer 'no'. We then realized
that we needed to answer not with a gut reaction but to be
able to support Biblically whatever we said.

Our answer is still 'no', but here is why we feel confident with
that response. Sometimes good ideas or things become sul-
lied when they are misused or when they are associated with
something bad. A physical example might be if a person is
served overcooked, mushy and unpalatable vegetables while
growing up. If they shun veggies and miss out on wonderful tastes and nutrition, it is not because something is wrong
with vegetables, but because it was presented in an awful way.

Because of the racist, hate-filled way it was used in the United States, the concept of 'separate but equal' was vilified. Partially because of this abuse, as well as a mistaken idea of what
equality means, our society has great difficulty with making
distinctions at all.

God has no such problems. He encourages distinction. In the Bible, the first-born was set apart with certain unique privileges and responsibilities. After the episode of the Golden Calf, most of those distinctive rules were transferred to the priests from the tribe of Levi. To this day, descendants of Aaron the High Priest have obligations and limitations on their behavior that the rest of Israel does not share. They are also accorded extra respect, for example being called up to the Torah in synagogue before other members of the congregation. In this way, they are 'set aside,' but that is very different than being loved more or less.

Similarly, God expects different things from men and women and those of us who believe that He designed the world to work best when we follow His ways would do well to retain those distinctions. If human beings abuse that concept, and treat women in a less loving way, it doesn't reflect on God's reality, but on human weakness and stupidity.

We hope this gives you a starting point as to why we feel that you can be confident in God's love for each and every one of us, both female and male.

Never hesitate to ask questions,

Rabbi Daniel and Susan Lapin

61.
How To Discern Truth

Are there tests/questions for some ideas/concepts to see if they are true?

Toda Raba (thank you),

Jonathan

Jonathan,

Isn't it interesting that throughout history the idea of being uncertain about truth is a common theme? Much of Greek tragedy revolves around the oracle at Delphi that gave cryptic answers that were misinterpreted. In other periods as well, we see many examples of good people who thought they were doing the 'right thing', when hindsight makes it clear that they were sorely mistaken in their actions.

Evidently, there is no foolproof method by which to discern the truth. However, we do need to make an effort and there are a number of clues that spring from ancient Jewish wisdom and the Hebrew language. In God's language, the Hebrew word for truth, EMeT is composed of the first, middle and last letter of the alphabet. So often, we only see part of a situation rather than the whole story. In seeking truth, we need to make sure that we have an entire breadth of knowledge. We need to trace the seeds of an issue back to their very beginnings, not skip any important details along the way and finally conclude with the end of the story – that may mean making honest projections into the future.

For this reason, we should be wary of 'new' ideas that are presented as truths. Often, a little exploration will reveal that they are gussied up remakes of concepts that brought misery in the past. For us, the Bible with traditional transmission of its meaning stands as the most trusted guide.

Best wishes,

Rabbi Daniel and Susan Lapin

62.
What Makes Food Kosher and Why Is It Important?

As one of your Christian readers, I have learned many fascinating life lessons as you explain the Old Testament scriptures. I am glad to be one of your students.

One topic I have always wanted to know more about what makes food kosher and its importance. I see kosher foods often in my own pantry, but would appreciate your explanation.

Tom D.

Dear Tom,

We don't want to ignore your question, but neither is it possible for us to treat it adequately in a short response. Consider what follows as a basic introduction.

All vegetables and fruit are kosher (though bugs are not so these items need to be properly cleaned). Kosher thus mostly revolves around meat and dairy. Only certain animals may be eaten—that's rule number 1. Number 2 is that permitted animals must be slaughtered in a specific manner, one feature of which is that it is designed to terminate consciousness as rapidly as possible. Finally, no meat or meat-derived food may be cooked or eaten together with any dairy or dairy-derived food. Cookware, tableware and many other items are designated as meat or milk, not both.

There are two very common misconceptions about kosher food. Unfortunately, an overwhelming number of people think that food is kosher because it is blessed by a rabbi. If that was so, we would, after a very quick blessing, be eating at some wonderful (we are told) non-kosher restaurants. Kosher foods are actually under rabbinical supervision to see that all the ingredients and processes used match the dietary requirements. In today's complex society, supervising rabbis need to know chemistry, biology and engineering to understand exactly what goes into an ingredient. These supervising rabbis travel to the farthest reaches of earth to research each minute component that goes into a product. An example of what might make a food unkosher would be an ingredient that has a non-kosher animal fat as part of its make-up. Alternatively, since we don't mix meat and milk, even kosher-based animal fat in a product with milk components would be unacceptable.

The second misconception is that kosher supervision raises the price of a product for everyone. Certainly, kosher supervision can be expensive. However, companies that pay for the supervision do so because they sell more by being kosher and so compensate for that cost by making additional profit. Not only Jews who keep kosher but also people such as vegans and those with allergies rely on the kosher supervision to have confidence in what they are eating.

Since eating is such a big part of our lives, it is hard to overestimate the practical and spiritual consequences of keeping kosher. Unfortunately, we don't have room to begin skimming the surface on that part of your question.

Rabbi Daniel and Susan Lapin

63.
Is Judaism the Oldest Continuous Culture in the History of the World?

You mentioned in an answer to another question that Judaism is the oldest continuous culture in the history of the world. Aren't Asian cultures older?

Warmly,

Michael L.

Dear Michael,

Your question is often asked and we are grateful you give us the opportunity to respond.

The only two Asian cultures that are potential candidates are India and China. Hindu scholars are among the first to acknowledge that Hebrew culture significantly predates theirs. As a matter of fact, in accordance with the writings of Menashe ben Israel, the 17th century distinguished Dutch rabbi and Torah scholar, they confirm that Hindu culture and much of the Hindi language derives from the sons of Abraham (through Keturah) some of whom are buried in well-known shrines along the banks of the Ganges. This is of course why the highest Hindu caste is a Brahma or son of Abraham—a term for those who trace their lineage back to one of those sons. This also explains the remarkable closeness between Hindi and Hebrew with many shared words.

There has been considerable evolution of the Hindi language over the centuries much as there has been in English. For instance, Middle English of Shakespeare's time is hard enough for today's casual English reader. Old English of 400 years earlier is quite impenetrable. Similarly, today's Hindi reader would have trouble with the language of 1,000 years ago let alone twice that time

The same situation is found in China where there is such a complicated language with so many letters or symbols that a conventional western style computer keyboard is overwhelmed. The reason is that each succeeding dynasty superimposed its culture on the preceding, rather than continuing or replacing it. Nobody in China today can casually pick up a manuscript from even 1,500 years ago and read it. However, the youngster on the street in Tel Aviv has little trouble reading and comprehending the words of the prophet Jeremiah from well over two millennia earlier.

For these reasons, we remain firm in our conviction that the only continuous 3,000 year-old culture in which language, religious belief, lifestyle tradition, marriage, divorce, and death practices, along with other customs such as circumcision, phylacteries and so on have remained utterly unchanged is the Hebrew. There truly is nothing even remotely comparable among the world's many cultures.

Rabbi Daniel and Susan Lapin

64.
I Just Found Out That My Mother was Jewish!

I was raised as a Christian by my English mother. Just before she died I found out that she was Jewish and born in Germany. I was told that her father committed suicide and that by some means her mom and she were able to get passports (Visas) out of Germany around 1937 or so. My mother told me that her father had dared to make a Nazi pay rent and other things which didn't please those coming to power.

Do you know some good references about that time that would give me a better understanding of how the Jews perceived things and what really happened at that time. I am curious why my mother would become a Protestant when she was safe in England during WWII as I had heard that many Jewish people tried to become Christians to save themselves and their children. Thank you for reading this email.

Peter W.

Dear Peter,

You are in good company. Over the past few years, as the generation that was young during World War II passes away, we have heard numerous stories such as yours. So many people are finding out that their mother or father was born Jewish.

We cannot presume to put ourselves in the situation of those making decisions during those dark years. You say that your mother was 'safe in England' yet the fear that Hitler would invade England and the rest of the world was a very real one.

Too many Jews know the cost of being Jewish (persecution and hatred in many times and many places) without perceiving the value. It isn't hard to understand the thinking of someone who, after the W.W. II years, sees becoming and declaring oneself as a Christian to be a way to shield future generations. Particularly if with the dislocation of war, he or she can pretend never to have had Jewish blood, the temptation must have been overwhelming.

While some people convert to Judaism as a deliberate choice, anyone with a Jewish mother is born Jewish, much as you are born a member of a family. That means that people perceive themselves as Jewish and are perceived as such by others (such as the Nazis) regardless of whether they know anything of their heritage. If all you know about Judaism is that being a member of this 'family' makes people want to kill you—and your children—it is not hard to understand your mother's actions.

Hope this is helpful,

Rabbi Daniel and Susan Lapin

65.
Is the Sabbath of Today in Continuity with the Sabbath of Moses' Day?

Do you know if the current accounting of the days of the week are unbroken and continuous from the days of Moses?

In other words, is Saturday (the Sabbath) of today still in continuity from the Sabbath of Moses' day?

John

Dear John,

We'll match you and raise you one. Not only has the counting of the seven days of the week been continuous since the days of Moses, but it has been continuous since Adam and Eve celebrated the first Sabbath the day after they were created, about 5,000 years ago.

We are so used to the idea of a week consisting of seven days that we don't stop to think what an illogical idea it is. We discuss the astounding implications behind the seven day week in our audio CD, *The Ten Commandments*. Once you realize how unlikely it is that mankind would have naturally developed a seven day week, you can understand the importance of the Sabbath and its ramifications.

It is inconceivable that humanity could have lost the cycle of days without being aware of it. Both Adam and Noah were in direct contact with God, and since Noah's days, there have been too many people in too many places for a mistake to creep in unnoticed.

Rabbi Daniel and Susan Lapin

66.
Do You Believe in Divine Healing?

How do you feel about divine healing?

Melanie B.

Melanie,

Perhaps we don't understand the question, but we don't know of any healing that isn't Divine. Each and every moment of life is a gift from God. See Exodus 15:26, "...for I am the Lord that heals you."

Having said that, we do believe that we should appreciate and take advantage of the wisdom that God has given to man, which allows him to combat illnesses. Doctors and scientists can serve as God's messengers.

We are also taught that the body and soul both need to be kept healthy—some call this holistic health. It is very difficult to keep our bodies healthy if our souls are sick.

When things happen repeatedly we begin to lose sight of how miraculous they are. We should work on being constantly aware that only Divine Guidance allows our bodies to work in ways that we take for granted.

Stay healthy,

Rabbi Daniel and Susan Lapin

67.
Why Do Jewish Men
Cover Their Heads?

I so much treasured your wisdom at the recent Wallbuilder's Conference. My grandson and I are visiting together and I have been sharing some of the wisdom I gained from you. He asked a question that I could not answer. Can you tell me why you wear the hat on your head? Do you wear it all the time?

Peggy M.

Dear Peggy,

We very much enjoyed being at the Wallbuilder's Conference and look forward to returning.

Jewish men have an obligation to cover their heads, be it with a hat, a baseball cap or other piece of haberdashery. In Jewish gift stores, you can purchase a flat, round covering known as a "kipah" or "yarmulke," which translate respectively as "covering" and "fear of the King".

The idea behind this has to do with the power of the intellect or the head. Using one's head can lead to life-saving inventions, prosperity, and myriad other fantastic outcomes. However, men (more than women) easily become full of themselves and convinced of their own brilliance. The same intellect that can lead to good can also lead to disaster. Neither I.Q. nor academic degrees confer good values.

The covering is certainly not foolproof by any means, especially when it turns into a meaningless source of ethnic dress, but it is meant to serve as a constant reminder that the One above us should be consulted in all our plans.

Rabbi Daniel and Susan Lapin

68.
The Significance of Every Name and Word in the Bible

Rabbi Daniel & Susan Lapin,

I noticed that the Bible sometimes refers to God in the lineage of Israel as the God of Abraham, Isaac, and Jacob and sometimes as the God of Abraham, Isaac and Israel. Is there significance to this?

Rozlyn F.

Rozlyn,

What a great question! There is significance not only to every name and word in the Bible, but to every letter.

We will up your ante by telling you that the Hebrew name for Jacob, Ya'akov, even has a variant spelling in specific places in the Bible. Unlike Abraham and Sarah, who, once they receive new names are called only by those new names, Jacob is called both Jacob and Israel throughout his life, as you noticed.

To get you started analyzing this unusual phenomenon, you can make a list of the different places each name is used. You will see a pattern emerging whereby Jacob tends to refer to the individual head of his family and Israel refers to the head of the future nation. Focusing in on small details is a wonderful way to gain more from Bible study.

Happy hunting,

Rabbi Daniel and Susan Lapin

69.
How Does an Agnostic Explore Faith?

I am Jewish by birth, but for many years have been an agnostic. I think that faith is more heart based than head. How does someone develop faith or all of a sudden believe in God?

Brian K.

Dear Brian,

Let's look at how we use the word "believe". At one point, my children believed in the tooth fairy. That was a heart (and pocketbook) based belief. They now believe in gravity, even though most of them don't have the physics background to back up their beliefs.

The two beliefs are quite different. We disagree with you that faith is more heart based than head. While loving God is heart based, that can only come after knowing there is a God. Maimonides said that every Jew has an obligation to KNOW that God exists. That is quite different from believing in Him.

If you are serious about questioning your agnosticism, the place to start is by learning. There are many authentic resources available today both around the world, in Israel and on line, including our own resources. An honest attempt to learn more will pay great dividends.

Rabbi Daniel and Susan Lapin

70.
The Meaning of Numbers in Scripture

I remember hearing that numbers have significant meaning in Hebrew scripture and Jewish tradition. It strikes me that there are certain numbers that appear numerous times in the Bible. For example, 40 days and nights of rain preceded the flood – and 40 years of wandering in the desert preceded the entry into Israel.

What - if any - is the significance of these numbers and is there a method to understanding the relevance of numbers overall when reading the Bible?

Karen C.

Karen,

You are raising an excellent point. Numbers in the Bible are very significant. In fact, the end of the Passover Seder features a song, "Who knows one?" that goes through the numbers 1-13.

While many mistake this for a children's song, it is declaring a major piece of Jewish thought; that numbers matter. As God's hand is behind history, it is not at all a coincidence that there were 40 days of rain, 40 years in the desert, or that a surprising number of Israel's kings reigned for 40 years. A number of our resources focus on different numbers.

Keeping track of various numbers as you read the Bible, maybe even making a chart, will give you much food for thought. We'll start you off with one fascinating example. Sarah lived for 127 years and King Achashverosh, in the Scroll of Esther, reigned over 127 lands. The number serves to connect these stories, bringing out otherwise easily overlooked ideas.

Rabbi Daniel and Susan Lapin

71.
My Husband Left Me Because of Faith

I have always respected you, your organization and your re-
ligion though I am a Christian. It is long past the occurrence
but I would like to know your full thinking of the following: I
married a secular Jew.

After 21 years of marriage, he drifted toward Orthodoxy
and finally revealed he would have to leave me so he could
practice the Orthodox Jewish religion. He subsequently did,
remarried an Orthodox Jewish woman and lives in an Or-
thodox community. Why was it necessary that he leave?

Mary K.

Dear Mary,

Firstly, we want to acknowledge that this was a painful experience for you. We hope we can answer your question in a
sensitive way.

For seventeen years, I (Rabbi Lapin) served as the founding
rabbi of the congregation that Michael Medved and I started
in Venice, CA. (Susan appeared shortly after the synagogue
started.) Our synagogue attracted many Jews who had been
brought up in ignorance of their religion. Not surprisingly,
the majority of them were young, since youth is a time for
searching and flexibility.

Two older couples joined our group. Each had been married

for many years. We stood in awe of their ability to totally change their established lifestyles as well as their belief systems at an advanced age. At one point, both couples were invited to be guests on a well-known national talk show to discuss the topic of intermarriage. On the show, one of the men mentioned how despite being brought up with no more than an ethnic identity as a Jew, he did get the message from his parents that he should marry Jewish. (This was very common in an earlier generation.) He said that when he and his wife were young, they would have thought anyone who suggested they might one day be observant Jews, was bonkers. However, as their lives unfolded and they were exposed to the Torah, they were able to make the journey to religious observance together. He suggested that it was important to marry someone of the same faith, even if you were irreligious, because you never knew where life might take you.

This gentle man was booed by the overwhelmingly young audience. While the rudeness was inexcusable, his is indeed a weak argument in today's world. Nevertheless, he was revealing a truth that affected your own life.

You see, serious Torah Judaism directs every facet of one's life. It governs what and how you eat, where and when you travel and work, and even the intimate life of husband and wife. It is much more than a matter of going to synagogue once or twice a week or saying some prayers on a daily basis. It is impossible to live a full life with someone who is not committed to the same path. Furthermore, there is a specific commandment against marrying outside the faith.

When you married, you and your husband were unwittingly unaware that one's relationship with God could truly be the most important factor in one's life. If your husband's soul was pulling him towards a sincere and passionate relationship with God and His Torah, there was no way for that to be compatible with a sincere and passionate relationship with you. Unless your conscience and soul led you to a conversion independent of your marriage, there simply was no way for you to stay together.

As painful as the separation was, it was a consequence of the unfortunate truth that when you marry a secular Jew you are really marrying a secular person of Jewish descent. If that secular identity is replaced, he or she is no longer the person you married.

We pray that you have made a happy and successful new life for yourself.

Rabbi Daniel and Susan Lapin

72.
Aren't Biblical Punishments Too Harsh?

I am curious... How do Jewish people view the seemingly harsh "commandments" in the Hebrew bible?

When is the last time someone got stoned for cheating on their wife or disobeying their parents?

Joe L.

Dear Joe,

We can't tell you how Jewish people – who are a disparate, diverse and far-flung group- collectively view anything. There are those Jews who take Jewish values seriously and there are those who don't. However, we can tell you what those Jewish values are and pass on the Torah knowledge we were taught.

It is interesting that you specifically cite the death penalty that is mentioned for a disobedient son. Ancient Jewish wisdom tells us that no Jewish court ever applied the death penalty in such a case. The parameters mandated in terms of warnings that must be given, the way the parents must have functioned, and actions the child must take in front of witnesses, make it almost impossible to fulfill the terms required for the death penalty.

In that case, what is the purpose of the words in Deuteronomy 21?

Moral relativism is dangerous for a society. If a poll was taken today or a debate hosted among the nation's "intellectuals" to discuss those actions that damage a civilization, we doubt if people would rank adultery on a par with murder. God's book tells us that He thinks differently. Furthermore, recognizing that a certain behavior makes one worthy of the death penalty, even if it is not imposed, gives a clear message of how unacceptable and threatening to society that behavior is.

We don't view those types of punishments as harsh but rather as providing a framework of moral structure to proscribe extremely destructive behavior, so that we can live among each other in peace and prosperity.

Rabbi Daniel and Susan Lapin

73.
The Torah and the Declaration of Independence

Which particular verses of the Torah, if any, most strongly support Jefferson's claim in the Declaration of Independence that natural law provides us all with self-evident, unalienable rights?

Robert W.

Dear Robert,

What a great question for a Fourth of July celebration.

The short answer is that the reality of God, or as Jefferson would have called Him, the Creator, provides the basis for the idea of unalienable rights.

In our audio CD, *The Ten Commandments: How Two Tablets Can Transform Your Life* we ask why what we call the Ten Commandments is referred to most frequently in the Bible as the "Two Tablets." Couldn't God have given them on one tablet? Furthermore, why are they composed of those specific ten items when other important ideas such as setting up a legal system or giving charity aren't listed there?

We explain that there are really five principles with two examples of each principle. Principle #1 matches with #6, #2 pairs with #7 and so on. Every concept needed for human interaction flows from these five principles. If you leave off the principles that refer to our relationship with God, the principles that refer to human interaction will not endure. America's founding fathers understood this well.

We hope you gain a greater appreciation of the origins of our great country,

Rabbi Daniel and Susan Lapin

74.
How Can I Make Mealtime Matter?

Out of the many questions I could ask of profound import, I have decided on this obscure one: You teach a lot on the Sabbath and Sabbath meals but what about the meals on the other 6 days?

Is it just a 'do your own thing' or are there specific guidelines for those meals? This inquiring mind wants to know!

Matthew M.

Dear Matthew,

In their trade magazines, the fast food industry refers to their customers as 'grazers.' Note that the identical language is used for how cows eat. The Jewish attitude highlighting the holiness of food and meals couldn't be more different.

Since the destruction of the Temple over 2,000 years ago, ancient Jewish wisdom has seen the family meal table as the replacement for the altar. While Sabbath and holiday meals have an additional holiness to them, every time one eats is a special opportunity and must be transformed into a holy and special occasion.

Animals eat for physical sustenance. People should eat for both physical and spiritual reasons. A great deal of what we consider good table manners, such as using cutlery, chewing with our mouths closed, or dozens of other conventions, are all attempts to distinguish our eating from that of animals.

The Torah commands us to say a blessing before eating or drinking and again after finishing eating. There are different blessings depending on the specific type of food. While, unfortunately, many of us hastily mumble off the blessing as we race through our day, ideally each time we eat should focus our attention onto our Provider. Grabbing something out of the fridge and stuffing it in our mouths as we race out the door doesn't really fit in the picture.

Meals are times not just for appreciating God, but also for bonding with people. Even giving someone else the opportunity to answer amen to your blessing is a wonderful thing. Speaking words of Torah around the table elevates the meal further. Many studies emphasize that children who regularly participate in family meals have higher levels of physical, emotional and spiritual well-being. This comes as no surprise to anyone raised with a Biblical concept of food.

Happy mealtime,

Rabbi Daniel and Susan Lapin

75.
Holding a Grudge

I have a friend of the Jewish faith who interviewed someone for a job. He said the person's skills and personality were perfect for the position, but was not going to offer him the job because he was Egyptian. When I inquired as to why he said, "They held my people captive for 400 years." I thought he was joking and he got upset with me because he was serious.

It is hard for me to believe that he was taught this at Synagogue. How does this type of thought continue over thousands of years?

Rebecca S.

Dear Rebecca,

We found your letter quite interesting although we think your question wasn't the right one to ask. You made a common mistake, which is to make an assumption about a group based on your experience with one member of that group. "This type of thought" doesn't continue over thousands of years – it is actually the first time we've heard anything of this sort.

More to the point, your friend's view is in direct contradiction to the Bible. Deuteronomy 23:8 states, "...do not spurn an Egyptian for you were a stranger in his land." It is, of course important to understand why Jews are prohibited from spurning the Egyptian even though Israel was not in Egypt for a vacation but rather as slaves. That lies outside the scope of your question so we'll devote a future Thought Tools to answering that question. Nonetheless, the verse in Deuteronomy does contradict your friend's approach.

We do know Jews who won't buy German products, especially if the companies were active supporters of the Third Reich. We understand that emotional reaction, particularly for survivors and their children. As the Nazi years move into history we are sure that will fade away. We would argue that it should. All of us need to find a balance between remembering the past and not letting the past destroy our future. In Judaism, we annually observe a three-week period when we specifically focus on past national catastrophes and suffering. That means that there are forty-nine weeks (with scattered exceptional days) when we celebrate the past or plant our feet firmly in the present and the future. Perhaps that is one secret of continued Jewish success.

You now know more of Jewish thought on this topic than your friend does,

Rabbi Daniel and Susan Lapin

76.
Is There Anything Wrong
with Cremation?

I am a Christian and have considered cremation. Is there anything wrong with cremation?

Nancy A.

Dear Nancy,

We hope you'll understand that while we love teaching what the Torah says we are not comfortable telling you or any Christian how to act. May we recommend that you discuss this with a respected mentor and/or clergy from your own faith?

We can tell you that in Torah Judaism, proper treatment of the body after death is crucial. This is defined as burial in the ground, just as God told Adam toward the end of Genesis chapter 3. This is so important that even if one's parents expressed their wishes to be cremated, their children may not carry out those wishes. The idea is that after death, the parents will have entered a World of Truth and will be appalled that they ever wanted to do something counter to God's law. As such, giving them a proper burial is actually following their final wishes.

When the soul leaves the body at the time of death, the body's purpose for being no longer exists. However, as the vehicle that allowed the soul to interact with the world, it requires special treatment. Part of that treatment requires a gradual return to the earth via burial rather than the abrupt return via cremation.

In addition, resurrection of the dead is a central tenet of Judaism. Choosing to treat the body as if it will never be needed again could be seen as rejecting that belief.

You might find it interesting that a Torah scroll and other holy writings as well as printed prayer books and Bibles are never thrown out. They are also buried in the ground.

Rabbi Daniel and Susan Lapin

77.
The Implications
of the Zodiac Signs

*I recently purchased the Day for Atonement CD and I was
quite disappointed when you were speaking on horoscopes.
My disappointment arose when Rabbi Lapin did not name or
go through the entire zodiac. Are the few mentioned the only
ones represented on the Jewish calendar?*

Colotta T.

Dear Colotta,

We appreciate your compliment; at least, we think it was a
compliment. As our *Day for Atonement* CD program specifically teaches about a unique time of the year, we focused
only on the Zodiac signs for that period. One of our great
and constant frustrations, along with the rest of humanity,
is how we face time and space limitations. We always have
more to teach than we have room for, whether it is in our
weekly Thought Tools, our audio CDs, books, live appear-
ances or our TV show. The wonderful side of that is that we
can spend our whole lives growing and learning. God's message to us through Scripture is infinite.

Recorded in ancient Jewish wisdom are details of the zodiac
signs as taught by Abraham. Not in the silly manner found
in newspaper or magazine horoscope columns but with deep
and authentic understanding that certain times are more

conducive to certain activities than other times are. Judaism operates mostly on a lunar calendar and Jews are meant to be always aware of what Hebrew month it is and which phase of the moon's cycle we are in. The reason astrological periods do not correspond precisely to months like January or September is that they are aligned with the lunar month just like the Hebrew calendar.

Each Jewish holy day relates to the zodiac sign for that lunar month. Understanding the implications of the sign helps us to understand what spiritual muscle we should be building during that period.

Thanks for asking,

Rabbi Daniel and Susan Lapin

78.
Is Alcohol Acceptable?

In many Christian churches, they frown upon drinking alcoholic beverages. Did God allow the Jewish people to drink alcohol?

Thanks,

Bobbye Jean M.

Dear Bobbye Jean,

Wine has a special place in Judaism, and we are actually commanded to drink it on the Sabbath and holidays. That beverage even has a unique blessing. While grape juice can be substituted if someone doesn't tolerate alcohol, wine is considered on a higher level. At the same time, Judaism severely frowns upon drunkenness.

In general, the Torah presents a guide for living that elevates physical desires into spiritual expressions. When physicality and materialism downgrade people instead of uplifting them, we are seen as rejecting God's gifts.

Sex within the boundaries of marriage isn't merely tolerated but celebrated. On the other hand, misuse of sex in cases such as adultery or incest is severely dealt with. Being prosperous is seen as a wonderful blessing; but there are dozens of laws sculpting how one acts with one's money. We are intended to rejoice in the natural beauty of the world and in doing so draw closer to our Creator, but harshly warned against worshipping nature.

We are expected to enjoy the benefits of wine or other alcohol while never allowing it to control us. We humans have a tendency to move towards extremes, whether in the direction of being too ascetic or too licentious. The Torah provides a path where taking pleasure in the delights of this world serves as a means to our spiritual growth.

Cheers,

Rabbi Daniel and Susan Lapin

Questions & Answers
About Friends

79.
Why Are Religious People
So Hypocritical?

I was a Christian. I've gone to several churches, of various denominations. In each one, I found that people in positions of trust were nothing more than lying, power-hungry people. They used religion and their positions as a way to control people.

Many of the people I know who profess to be Christians are exactly the same; they live their lives to judge, control and proclaim they are "better" than others. They use the Bible as a weapon.

As a result, I find myself actually feeling anger whenever I hear someone proclaim they are Christian. The thought of Church angers me. I immediately feel animosity towards any religious people. Yet for all that, I know something is missing in my life. I still believe in God. I know I don't live my life the way God wants, yet am so turned off against Church, Christians and religion that I feel I have abandoned it.

Am I destined to live a life without God, running from his teachings because of my feelings about his followers?

Leigh

Dear Leigh,

There are so many different levels on which we read your

179

comments. It is perfectly normal to hold those close to us to a higher accountability than those farther from us. We are more embarrassed and angered by our parents than our friends' parents, by our countrymen than by those from other countries, at politicians who are supposed to share our values than those who oppose them and so forth. We can be quite unreasonable, actually. Is it possible that you are looking for Christians to be perfect people? If so, you are setting your search up for failure.

Without intending to trivialize your pain, we remember our response when people would sometimes decline our invitations to worship with us in the Southern California synagogue it was our privilege to lead. They'd indignantly decline our invite explaining, "Synagogues are always filled with hypocrites." Our response? Always the same: "If only perfect people attended synagogue, the place would be empty. The good news is that we won't be shocked to hear that you too have flaws." Your question however is different. You're obviously not merely trying to find an excuse for not affiliating. You express sadness about not having a faith family.

There are certainly corrupt and controlling religious leaders, as there are by the way, corrupt and controlling politicians, teachers, social workers and doctors. However, there are also leaders full of integrity and authentic spiritual welcome. We've met many of them. If you are only finding one type then perhaps you need to figure out how to seek in a different way.

A wonderful story is told of a man sitting on the outskirts of a town. Along comes a traveler who says, "I'm thinking of relocating. What types of people live in this town?"

The man answers, "What are the people like in the town you

are leaving?"

The traveler replies, "They are nasty, selfish and dishonest."

"Well, the people in this town are just like that," the man responds.

A short while later another traveler passes by, also looking to move.

"I'm thinking of relocating. What types of people live in this town?" he asks.

The local man (the same one as above) answers, "What are the people in your town like?"

"They are wonderful! Warm, honest and caring."

"The people in this town are just like that," comes back the response.

We certainly don't want to be hurtful and we know nothing about you other than your letter. Yet we think it is worth exploring if it is possible that there is a grain of truth in the above tale that might apply to your search. Above all, keep the search alive in your heart. Ceasing to search is fatal.

Wishing you success,

Rabbi Daniel and Susan Lapin

80.
Why Won't My Co-worker
Invite Me for Shabbat?

Yesterday, I asked an Orthodox Jewish co-worker in another department with whom I'm somewhat friendly with if he observes the Sabbath, and he responded that he does. I then asked if it was okay if I attended one at his home with him and his family, and he says that it is not allowed because I'm considered an outsider. I was sort of perplexed because I thought that if I was there as an observer then what is the harm?

Please let me know if this is in fact true. I do love ancient Jewish customs and the Jewish people although I am a Christian. Thank you in advance for your time and consideration of the question.

Natalie S.

Dear Natalie,

You must have taken your co-worker by complete surprise with your request. Most Jews and even many observant Jews are lamentably uninformed about Christian America and would be shocked to hear how interested many Christians are about Jewish customs.

We obviously don't know your co-worker, but for many Jews the Shabbat is enjoyed as only a family day. Sadly (in our opinion), they don't think of opening their homes even to

183

others in their own synagogue or neighborhood, let alone to non-observant Jews or people of other faiths. Having never thought about it, they might feel uncomfortable with an 'outsider' at the Shabbat table and perhaps even put on the spot having to explain some of the Sabbath customs and observances they are practicing. Your coworker might have even understood your request as asking to move in for 25 hours.

We're sorry you got that response and you certainly shouldn't feel that your request was out of line. After all, if you don't ask there isn't even a chance of getting a positive answer! You might even have given your co-worker some food for thought and opened him up to a new way of thinking. Of course, each of us is entitled to decide what to do in our own homes and he has every right not to welcome you as company, but it isn't a case of being "allowed" or not. In our own case, our seven children all agree that our weekly guests (including many of our Christian friends) have enormously enhanced the Sabbath meals at which they have kindly joined us.

All the best,

Rabbi Daniel and Susan Lapin

81.
What is the Biblical Concept
of Community?

*I'm a doctoral candidate in a Philosophy of Theology pro-
gram writing a dissertation. I'm attempting to answer the
question, "What is the biblical concept of community?"*

*More than understanding its historical expression I am seek-
ing to show how its value is critical to humanity in contem-
porary culture. What insights are found in the Torah for
defining and living in community? Thank you for your con-
tribution into my life through Thought Tools.*

Roderick L.

Dear Roderick,

It might take a dissertation of our own to answer that question – and that is something that will not fit in the space we
have here. We'd like to suggest two avenues for you to explore.

Firstly, Jewish communal prayer depends on the presence of
what is known as a 'minyan.' This means a gathering of ten
Jewish men, and when a minyan is not present, many prayers
cannot be recited. While Judaism is most strongly centered
in the home, the minyan provides a community counterpart.

Secondly, Jewish survival throughout centuries has benefit-
ted from the prohibition on travel on the Sabbath. Susan
wrote a Musing, *Strangers and Friends*, a number of years

ago that spoke of how this practice creates communities.

When we recently published the second edition of our book, *Buried Treasure: Secrets for Living from the Lord's Language*, we added an entirely new chapter on the Hebrew words for community. The different words for community in Hebrew reveal (sometimes surprising) aspects of this important concept.

We wish you well in your studies,

Rabbi Daniel and Susan Lapin

82.
Helping a Friend Move Past
a Troubling Issue...

My friend's 1st husband died 12 years ago, so 6 years after, she married again. She still considers herself a widow and is upset with the first husband's family for not including her as a sister-in-law when his brother died. She has also included the deceased's last name as part of her last name (i.e. Jones-Smith).

Is this Scriptural or right?

Cherlyn P.

Dear Cherlyn,

You are raising so many issues, but the question that strikes us is why you are asking the question at all. If your friend is asking your advice, our suggestion would be to tell her that she must find someone with experience in these areas whose opinion she respects, and ask herself. This question deals with feelings and emotions, rather than case law. If she is not asking for your advice, may we humbly suggest that you look into your heart to see why you are so troubled by her actions?

When a marriage takes place, more than two individuals are involved. Ideally, two families merge. When the marriage ends because one spouse dies, there can still be a strong bond between the survivors, though technically, they might seem unrelated. When there is a subsequent remarriage, things can become even more complex. Each family is different and it is easy to offend and hurt each other if communication is not managed well and prioritized.

There is also the important subject of how your friend's feelings are affecting her new marriage. Again, each situation is unique and there are many factors such as children, which come into play. Surnames are a relatively recent addition to society and while they serve a purpose, they do potentially raise problems.

It sounds to us like your friend needs emotional support as she works through grief, loss and starting over. Sometimes the best thing a friend can do is honestly say that while she can give a hug and an ear, the issues that are causing pain are not ones she feels competent to comment on. As such, helping your friend to either move past the issue by not allowing her to rehash hurt feelings over and over with you, or encouraging her to discuss it with someone other than you, may be the best act of friendship.

Wishing you and your friend the best,

Rabbi Daniel and Susan Lapin

83.
Could My Feelings for
My Rabbi be Unhealthy?

I am a single woman of 41, never had any serious relation-
ship but always dreamed of love and never found it. I came
to a new congregation and I fell deeply in admiration with
my rabbi's wisdom. We had some very insightful debates on
Jewish issues, and he expressed that he considers me a very
special and beautiful soul and mind. Nonetheless, I feel he
might also feel a deeper attraction for me, and I am very
much afraid that my deep admiration for him might turn
into something else. But he is married, of course. I know I
should avoid any contact and flee from the possibility of sin,
but at the same time, it is really hard for me to finally find
such a light and have to withdraw from him because the
want of each other's light could go out of control (but also
could not). What should I do?

Naomi

Dear Naomi,

What you should do is see red lights flashing and hear warn-
ing signals. We think that your writing to us confirms that
you already know that. Let's deal with facts rather than con-
jecture. You know how you are feeling. You cannot know
whether the rabbi feels similarly or not. It is possible that
you are noticing subtle signals coming from the rabbi; possibly even ones of which he is not aware. However, you might
be mistaking general warmth and kindness for something
more personal. His statement about a beautiful soul and

mind could certainly be an innocent one. Which of these is the truth is unknowable from what you wrote. What you do know is that you are trespassing very closely to violating the Tenth Commandment: Thou Shall Not Covet.

Even more worrying is another possibility. Perhaps the rabbi is indeed motivated by nothing but a pure eagerness to help and support someone he recognizes to be a beautiful person suffering from the pain of loneliness. However, spending time together, ostensibly for therapy and guidance, has more than once crystallized into something quite different which could shatter his life and postpone your happiness indefinitely.

God does not ask us to do anything that is impossible. Since in this commandment He charges us with controlling our thoughts, we must be able to do so. We would suggest that you work on refusing to let your mind dwell on any attraction you feel. You need to redirect your thoughts in another direction. At the same time, you should minimize conversation and contact with the rabbi. You definitely should not be discussing any personal matters with him or interact other than as part of a large group.

It is possible that you need to find another congregation, even one that will be less fulfilling. You certainly need to do that if at any point you feel the slightest boundary line is broached by the rabbi or alternatively if you are simply unable to do the tremendously difficult but enormously rewarding job of directing your thoughts in permissible and positive directions.

We wish you success in finding a life-mate in a blessed relationship,

Rabbi Daniel and Susan Lapin

84.
When Friends Don't See Eye to Eye
Because of Different Theologies

I have a friend who I thought of as a very close friend. Five years ago, she retired from her full time job as anesthesia nurse but kept her part time (Saturdays only) job at a local clinic. And that is how she referred to it - as a "clinic".

I recently was floored to find out that the clinic is not a health clinic as I had thought all these years. It is an abortion clinic and she is the anesthesia nurse in the clinic. I am a devout Roman Catholic and am wondering if I must give up my friendship with this woman or what my religious obligation is in this matter.

I found it very telling that she never told me the true nature of her work all of these years. She is a convert to Islam (for the past 40 years). I am only thankful that I now live on the opposite coast of the country from her but since I moved to the West Coast we have visited back and forth at least twice a year. I am grateful for any guidance you can give to me.

Barbara T.

Dear Barbara,

What a shock this must have been for you and what a difficult situation! Our guess is that your friend was sensitive to the idea that you would be pained by her activities and refrained from mentioning them for that reason. We personally do not know what the Muslim position on abortion is and whether your friend is acting in accordance with her faith or has reasons of her own to be uncomfortable with her workplace.

We would encourage you to seek personal guidance from your priest, but we do have some thoughts you might wish to consider. For your friendship to have thrived all these years, you both clearly were comfortable with acknowledging your different theologies. While, as a Roman Catholic, your position on abortion is deeply felt, this may be an area that she sees entirely differently. That doesn't mean you need to accept her view; but it is the reality.

After speaking to your priest, should you feel unable to continue the friendship, we think that you should explain your feelings to your friend rather than just trying to be unavailable and passively end the relationship. We all have lines that we simply do not cross (or should have such lines) and if this is one of yours, she should know that your position includes deep regret and pain but that you proudly follow the teachings of your faith.

We applaud you for not falling for the popular thinking that we must accept everyone's choices as to what is moral and right and what isn't. We each do need to have the courage to uphold certain standards and draw definite lines in the sand.

Please let us know what happens,

Rabbi Daniel and Susan Lapin

85.
Being Prickly or Positively Assertive

My best friend and husband are Jewish. I am often invited to social gatherings together with all of their Jewish friends. I have heard some of them talking about a person and then calling that person a "Wanna be Jew" (as if that were a bad thing). Recently my best friend told someone, in my presence, that I was a "Wanna be Jew." It bothered me and I don't know how to deal with this.

I admire and respect their faith and have been with them to celebrate some holidays. What do you think this means? Thank you.

Carol

Dear Carol,

We have to admit that we are not familiar with this phrase. Nevertheless, we think our advice on how to react would be similar to anyone who is uncomfortable with how someone speaks or acts to them.

We need a constant balance in our lives between being prickly and easily offended vs. being positively assertive. One of the maladies of our society is the way we jump to take offense and the ease with which we tend to attack people for innocuous statements, particularly individuals who are in the public arena.

However, especially with personal interactions, it is important to be up front if something is making you uncomfortable. Otherwise, you risk building a barrier in the relationship without giving the other party a chance to explain or change. In this case, you have a statement being repeated more than once so you can assume that it is deliberate rather than a careless usage of language. Since a good friend used it, it is safe to assume that she has no idea it could be bothering you.

Calmly ask your friend what she and her friends mean by that phrase. Tell her that you don't understand it, but it makes you feel bad. Our guess is that she will not find it easy to explain the phrase or it will make her do some self-analysis. Many Jews are ambivalent about their heritage and it is possible that your interest makes them feel somewhat embarrassed about how little they value their own background. Since it is making you feel awkward, we would expect her to stop using it and to become aware when her friends do, letting her steer their language in a different direction as well.

Rabbi Daniel and Susan Lapin

86.
Sharing Your Table with Friends and Strangers

In the book of Genesis, when the three visitors visit Abraham, it seems to me he really goes out of his way to welcome them and make a meal for them. Was that customary back then or did he know that those three men were someone special?

Andrea

Dear Andrea,

The answer to your two questions is, 'No and sort of'. Starting with your second one first, Abraham did not know they were angels at the point he invited them for a meal. However, he did know they were special – they were human beings (he thought) created in the image of God.

As for the answer to your first question, it was not at all customary to be on the constant lookout for guests and to treat them with warmth and great hospitality. This explains why Abraham is considered to represent the quality of chesed, or loving kindness. That trait is so intertwined with who he is that ancient Jewish wisdom tells us that if a person is sorely lacking in kindness and mercy he or she is not from the seed of Abraham.

It is partly in recognition of Abraham's hospitality that one of our great joys is to have guests join us for the Shabbat meals on Friday night and Saturday lunch. Jews everywhere keep this spirit alive by sharing their tables with friends and strangers.

As God's primary representative in the world, Abraham embodied the idea that recognition of God and respect for His creations are not ideas that can be separated. Just as he introduced those around him to monotheism, he also introduced the concept of cherishing all others, be they family or strangers, by means of actually doing wonderful things for them such as providing them with food.

All the best,

Rabbi Daniel and Susan Lapin

87.
Am I My Brother's Keeper?

Respectfully, I ask if it is possible that the original question by Cain, "Am I my brothers' keeper?" is answered No? In researching, I find the word keeper to mean his/her life is in my hands...it is not nor should it be. Could this be at least partially the reason why so many Jewish people go for the "social justice", Socialism etc.

Because the Bible speaks of helping others (I totally concur) and not letting the government "help" we must be as profitable as possible in order to help others. Socialism prevents and even thwarts this. Another view would be welcome if I am wrong. The overwhelming number of Jewish people who vote "liberal" has bothered me for so long especially since they are the ones who suffer the most when these dictatorial ways of governing are in place.

Thank you. Respectfully,

Faith M.

Dear Faith,

You ask a wonderfully important question. How can so many of the spiritual heirs to those who stood at the foot of Mt Sinai as God gave the Ten Commandments and the Torah be dedicated to the destructive policies of secular liberalism.

In short, we will tell you that many Jews who have become

secular liberals have adopted this as their entire belief system. Though they may say things like, "I'm proud to be Jewish," they have long ago abandoned the faith of Abraham, Isaac and Jacob and became ethnic Jews for whom the Torah is not the word of God and in no way binding upon humanity in general and Jews in particular.

You are correct that the Bible delineates exactly what our obligations to others are. There are both obligations and limitations in our responsibility towards our fellow man. And yes, being able to help others can only happen if each individual has money and possessions from which to give.

Incidentally, the Hebrew word in the phrase you cite, "Am I my brother's keeper?" is 'SHoMeR'. It is a nuanced word with specific levels of obligation in different circumstances. It does not automatically imply complete and total responsibility.

We hope this helps answer your question,

Rabbi Daniel and Susan Lapin

88.
I Took an Instant Dislike to Someone

I recently found myself in a very difficult situation dealing with someone I had never met but needed to correspond with over the phone. We clashed like oil and water and I really don't know why. I felt such hatred but I could not be pleasant with her at all. I am a very easygoing person and it takes a lot to get me angry but for some reason I clashed with her from the moment I said hello. I feel like I have let G-d down.

Can you please let me know why these feelings have taken control of me? I have asked other people if this ever happened to them and I have heard that it has to everyone at least once.

Thank you for your time,

Anita F.

Dear Anita,

What an intriguing question. We tend to agree with the people you asked that most of us have had the experience of taking an instant dislike to someone. That is really the mirror image of infatuation or feeling close to someone we barely know, based only on minimal contact. Whether it is a strong like or dislike, acting on those instincts tends to get us in trouble.

This can even happen with parents or teachers, and in those

199

situations the responsible adult needs to be extra zealous to overcome his or her impulses. In the case of a negative reaction, while we can sometimes put our finger on the offending factor—perhaps the person shares a name or looks like someone who harmed us—ancient Jewish wisdom suggests that we explore one more area as well.

The suggestion is that frequently what disturbs us about people is that we recognize in them a trait that we don't like in ourselves. For example, if we find ourselves illogically reacting negatively to someone who seems to "know it all," some honest introspection might force us to recognize that we share that tendency.

Whatever the reason for your reaction, we certainly don't disappoint God by being human. The situation you were in was a growth opportunity, and God places these opportunities in our path so that we may overcome the challenge. If you weren't successful in this particular case, you can be sure that more such occasions will come your way, as they do to us.

Best wishes,

Rabbi Daniel and Susan Lapin

89.
My Daughter Wants to Marry
Outside of the Faith

I am a Jewish parent. I have 3 children.

Two of my children have married within the religion. My youngest daughter is dating a Christian. She seems to be in love. My wife and I would prefer to see her marry within our religion. Her friend seems to be a very good guy, but not Jewish.

My daughter is 26 yrs old and an adult. She is torn between pleasing her parents and her love for her friend. How should we handle this situation?

Randall H.

Dear Randall,

This is one of those questions that is incredibly hard to answer without knowing you, your family and the young man in question. In fact, we can't really give an answer as much as raise questions for discussion.

In general, we think that making a success of marriage is so difficult that sharing a conception of God and His wishes is a tremendous advantage. However, we don't know if your daughter and her friend have a relationship with God, or if their respective views of Judaism and Christianity are more forms of ethnic identities or a question of whether they say

"Happy Hanuka" or "Merry Christmas" each December.

Does either religion have true value for the young couple or is it only, at best, their parents' thing? Why is your daughter torn? Are you and your wife saying, "We'd prefer you marry in our faith," or are you saying, "We love you, we have spent your entire life showing you how our religion affects every moment of our day and we are crushed that you are willing to betray our core identity." Is your daughter shocked to find out that you feel this way because from her viewpoint Judaism seemed way down on things you valued?

We would urge your daughter not to minimize the religious differences, and she should know that what seems unimportant in her twenties might be of major importance when she has children or as she gets older.

Marriage is such a large, life-changing decision, that we would encourage your daughter to make sure she knows what she is rejecting if she goes forward with this. Unfortunately, the majority of Jews are unfamiliar with most aspects of Judaism. We would think she should also explore exactly what her friend's beliefs are and how they affect his life and decision making. Is she willing to adopt his beliefs? If not, can she answer why not? How will that play out in life?

Perhaps your question is not what she should do, but how you should react. We'd say that you might want to explore what about Judaism is important to you and spend the next few years learning more so that your grandchildren, from all your children, will see that it is something of tremendous value that they would not be able to imagine abandoning.

Rabbi Daniel and Susan Lapin

90.
Does Being Assertive Mean Being Mean?

I recently was given a different responsibility at work and my co-worker said I wasn't mean enough? I know she meant I wasn't assertive enough.

Do you have any suggestions on how to set boundaries and still be what God intends us to be?

Carissa C.

Dear Carissa,

We agree that your co-worker probably wasn't suggesting that you should start puncturing her tires or writing nasty emails about her.

Why not take a lesson from Moses? In Numbers 12:3, we are told that he was more humble than anyone else. Yet, this humble man repeatedly threatened Pharaoh, dealt strongly with rebellion against his leadership (Korach), all while standing at the head of millions of people.

Ancient Jewish wisdom explains that Moses was fully cognizant of his many talents and attributes. Yet, he also knew that they were a blessing from God, not due to him. Even though he was in charge, he was just as subservient to the laws of the Torah and God's rules as everyone else was. Within those parameters he not only could, but also needed to, do what was necessary to get the job done.

You really answered your own question by recognizing that assertiveness and meanness are two completely different traits. If you are being advanced in your company then as long as you do not behave in a way that would embarrass you in front of God or negate Him, you have a responsibility to lead.

There are many ways to work on appearing more in control, including body language. When you stand, sit and speak in certain ways, you send a message not only to others, but also to yourself. Take some time to look into this area.

Good luck in your new position.

Rabbi Daniel and Susan Lapin

91.
How Do I Become a Mensch?

What does it mean to be a mensch? In trying times, a friend who was Jewish told me, "Be a mensch." I looked up the term and believe that it means a righteous person, but I don't think the dictionary quite explains it.

Is one born a mensch or does he simply rise to that status?

Richard S.

Dear Richard,

We're not surprised at your confusion. To tell you the truth, the vast number of Yiddish terms that have found their way into general American conversation and into the media astonishes us. We are sure that you are not the only one who doesn't understand terms like schlemiel, maven, chutzpah, macher, bris, kibbitz, and meshugah.

Firstly, you need to understand what Yiddish is. Unlike Hebrew, which is the Lord's language and the language in which He gave us the Bible, Yiddish is a language which was the daily vernacular for many Jews in Europe. The language is a combination of Hebrew and the languages of host countries such as Germany and France. Yiddish was not universal. Those Jews who lived in countries such as Greece and Turkey knew no Yiddish and instead spoke Ladino, a combination of Spanish, the local language and Hebrew. Yiddish was a language which allowed Jews in Poland, Germany, Russia and other countries to understand each other, with minor variations in words and pronunciations.

As Jews migrated to America, some words from the language began to enter American culture, particularly in places like New York where many Jewish immigrants lived. 'Mensch' is one of those words. It means a good person. A mensch is honest in business, shovels his elderly neighbor's sidewalk when it snows, goes out of his way to do favors for friends, etc., etc. No one is born a mensch and while it is admirable to be one, the word has no holy or sacred connotation.

And schlemiel means an unlucky fool, maven means expert, chutzpah is outrageous impudence, macher is an organizer-busybody, bris is circumcision, kibbitz means to joke around and someone who is meshugah is just nuts.

Rabbi Daniel and Susan Lapin

92.
Could My Friend Be Ruining Her Chances for Doing Better?

First of all, I want to let you know that I have been read-ing your Thought Tool which has been a blessing to me. It has given me new insights and helps me to further under-stand what God tell us in the Scriptures, when the meaning is translated from Hebrew. I want to thank you for sharing your knowledge and wisdom.

My question is about a good friend of mine, who works as a house cleaner, whom I respect and love.

When she is servicing the families that have hired her for cleaning, sometimes these families give her used things that they don't need any more. I consider this normal, but what concerns me is when they throw things away in the garbage that are still in good shape and she picks them out from the trash for her use.

Now I know that the Bible is full of promises of prosperity for us as children of God. I don't believe it is wise to pick things that others consider as useless from the trash. My question is; does this action actually bring poverty upon the life of a person who does this?

Thank in advance for your help.

Lily V.

Dear Lily,

Some actions are objectively good or bad. For example, no matter how you rationalize it, stealing from another person is wrong. Other actions can be good or bad for us depending on our attitude (as well as other factors). It sounds to us like this may be one of those cases where intention and attitude matter.

Feeling limited and static in one's life can bring or extend poverty. It is extremely important that we not confuse today's reality with tomorrow's opportunity. Human beings are not static or 'stuck' in whatever condition describes us now. If your friend feels degraded by taking items slated for garbage, then that may very well impact her future.

However, that is not necessarily the case. Her employers may feel uncomfortable giving her anything that is not in mint condition, thinking that it would insult her. She, however, may be delighted with a pair of pajamas that has a small rip or a pair of shoes with a scuff mark. She may see these items as part of a plan that allows her to manage her money and get out of debt or to put funds away for future needs. If when she collects these items, her attitude is one of gratitude rather than resentment and they make her feel more independent and capable, than we can't see any harm in it.

Wishing you and your friend a prosperous future,

Rabbi Daniel and Susan Lapin

93.
Accepting Responsibility Puts Us on the Path to Greatness

You wrote how important it is to be responsible for your actions. You concluded, "Accepting responsibility puts us on the path to greatness".

Given the opposite behavior in our highest political leaders - I have some serious doubt that this piece of advice really applies to the truly powerful in America in this decadent age. Perhaps in the afterlife these powerful prevaricators will get their just rewards, but on earth - the tactic of blaming others seems quite effective. How do you explain the success of those who successfully hold on to high office in the land and apparently prosper by blaming others?

Alan L.

Dear Alan,

We appreciate and share in the pain your letter reveals. It is demoralizing and frustrating to see people thrive in spite of awful behavior including not accepting responsibility. We were referring to moral and spiritual greatness. We certainly don't see election to high office as proof that successful candidates possess those qualities. Unfortunately, small people can wield great power.

While we firmly believe that everyone will receive his or her true reward and punishment in the afterlife, that isn't the whole picture either. Looking at humanity from a larger perspective, groups do not flourish over the long term when they choose leaders who are petty and small. Even over the span of an entire life, people with poor character traits seldom flourish. It is tempting to focus in on a short span of time (in relation to the world's history) or a specific individual and think that the world has turned upside down. In reality, we still would bet on Godly virtues and character traits for success in this – and the next - world.

Keep your chin up,

Rabbi Daniel and Susan Lapin

94.
Do I Need to Keep Promises to Friends?

I understand that there is provision made in one of the Jewish feasts to be forgiven and released from any foolish promise that has been made. Is this only for man to man or does it also pertain to any foolish promise(s) made to God?

Thank you for your consideration of this question.

Sara S.

Dear Sara,

We appreciate your question because we love clearing up misconceptions about Judaism. You are referring to a passage that is recited heading into Yom Kippur (Day of Atonement). It begins with the words, "Kol Nidrei" which mean, "all of my vows." This paragraph, which dates back to at least the 13th century is sung to a stirring tune and has been adapted and recorded by artists ranging from Ludwig von Beethoven and Max Bruch, all the way to Johnny Mathis.

The way you worded your question exactly reverses the premise of Kol Nidrei. The declaration, which annuls certain vows, only pertains to vows that do not affect another person. Jewish tradition takes swearing or taking oaths very seriously, and Kol Nidrei in no way allows anyone to betray a monetary or other promise to a fellow human being.

This passage became especially meaningful throughout history when Jews were given the choice of swearing allegiance to Catholicism or Islam on pain of death. While many accepted martyrdom, others swore falsely. Before Yom Kippur, Kol Nidrei served the purpose of declaring those insincere avowals of faith to be nullified.

Thanks for asking,

Rabbi Daniel and Susan Lapin

95.
When Friends Ask Tough Questions

Thank you so much for sharing all of your wonderful wisdom. I benefit greatly

I am a Christian who feels helpless to respond when I hear other Christians speak about how violent the Old Testament is. Can you offer some wisdom on this? I hear people questioning the violence and I'm afraid it puts them off to true commitment to their faith. Thank you!

Carolyn U.

Dear Carolyn,

We're so glad that you enjoy our teachings. We'd like to answer your question with an answer that springs from the Hagadah, the play book for the Passover Seder.

How violent is the Old Testament? Is it violent when it insists on compassion for the widow and orphan? Is it violent when it requires the lender to restore the borrower's pledge if he needs it to earn a living? Is it violent when it urges an army to offer peace to a besieged city?

Life is so good for most Americans, and so utterly secure that we sometimes assume that violence no longer exists other than perhaps occasionally in really bad parts of town or in really bad parts of the globe. We see violence as an aberration that can and must be stopped. The reality is quite different, and sadly, we are probably heading into more violent times.

If we announce to the world (or to our neighborhood) that we will never practice violence, we will suffer an increase of it. Only by fighting the bandit, executing the serial murderer, and defeating the invader, do we win the privilege of peace and tranquility. There is violence in the Bible because it is a part of the real world. Using harsh measures appropriately, as God does, enables more good people to live more tranquilly than they otherwise would. That having been said, we recommend you do not try to answer all questions. Here's why:

Each year on Passover Eve, we speak of four sons who ask questions. One son is wise; one wicked; one simple and one who doesn't know how to ask. Each human being is a composite of all four, in varying degrees, and we are encouraged to search ourselves to see in what proportion the four prototypes exist in us. The response to the wicked son seems callous and indifferent. We are told to spurn his question. Why?

The truth is that he is not asking a question, he is telling one. How do you tell a question? You do so by framing a belligerent statement in question form. In reality, you are making a declaration rather than seeking edification. An example of this might be, "Why do Republicans want to see old people starving on the street?" or a teenager saying to his or her parents, "Why do you never want me to be happy?" There is no way to answer those 'questions' until the one asking them is truly interested in a dialogue rather than delivering a diatribe. Trying to engage the questioner is a futile endeavor.

Seeking to understand the way in which God seems to be portrayed in Scripture, when it goes against our vision of God, is a valid and reasonable pursuit. However, if one is adamant about already knowing the answer (a la "because Republicans are cruel and evil" or "because you hate me") then there is no point in continuing the conversation.

Many years ago, in the days when meals were still served routinely on planes, our mother, Rebbetzin Lapin, received her kosher meal. Her seat mate informed her that he used to be kosher, but stopped following Jewish law after hearing of the Holocaust. After all, "How could a just and kind God allow the Holocaust to happen?" Further conversation revealed that he was twenty-five years old when the Holocaust became known, and had stopped keeping kosher at age twenty. Our very wise mother told him that seeking to understand God and His actions was worthy, but using God as an excuse for doing what one wanted to do anyway, was cowardly. (She was one tough lady.)

Your friends sound a bit like that airplane passenger. You cannot debate them on the issue. You can only wait for their hearts to open and be available to guide them to answers when they truly ask a question.

Rabbi Daniel and Susan Lapin

96.
Platonic Friendship
Outside of Marriage

Would you please give your opinion regarding the topic of platonic friendships outside of marriage?

Diana

Dear Diana,

Did we tell this story on the TV show?

A number of years ago we took our children hiking on a beautiful mountain trail not far from our home. On the way up we stopped at a viewpoint, and were joined by a group of parents and children heading down. The adults making up that party included many mothers and one father. As we shared the scenery, we chatted and discovered that the father wasn't married to any of the women. As a stay at home dad, he had responded to a notice seeking 'stay at home moms' who were looking to get together for trips, park outings and other activities.

This neighborhood gathering was obviously accustomed to explaining the co-ed make-up of the group, and the women and man seemed tickled at how progressive and modern they all were in expanding the concept to 'stay at home parents' rather than limiting it by gender. While it wasn't our place to comment to these friendly folk, in talking privately to each other, my husband and I agreed that this was courting trouble.

There are tremendously powerful forces that God built into this world, and one of the most powerful is that of sexual attraction. Properly used it enhances our lives immeasurably. However, improperly used, it is highly destructive.

We take as a given that the overwhelming majority of platonic friendships are initiated with the purest of intentions. Certainly, not all of them proceed to flirtatiousness or further improper behavior. However, there is no advance test that can tell you which relationships will end up leading to misery. Even if the friendship stays physically chaste, the emotional connection of one spouse to a person of the opposite sex is a form of betrayal.

Platonic relationships between single men and women have their own set of difficulties, among which is how to handle things when either friend gets married. Breaking down barriers between the sexes is one of those 'societal advancements' which has not lived up to its promise.

Rabbi Daniel and Susan Lapin

Is there any suggestion you might have to help a woman who seems to enjoy being negative all the time? She appreciates humor but for the most part, she is 'never having a good day.' She is often sick, has experienced cancer of the throat (but continues to smoke), and her husband is ill. Her sons live at home and don't contribute to their household much and it seems like she likes her chaos and depression.

I would like to see her experience a true faith in God which I feel would give her peace and freedom to enjoy all that she has and the strength to help others, but I'm not sure how I can do this.

Nanette

Dear Nanette,

You sound like a nice person. However, being a nice person doesn't give you supernatural powers. You don't say if this woman is a neighbor, relative or co-worker, but whether she is someone with whom you choose to interact or someone with whom you must interact, you still can't force her to be happier.

Even if her life is harder than you think, and there certainly could be facts of which you are unaware, you are correct that

219

her attitude is in her control. (Sometimes, it is the only thing that we can control.) It is incredibly frustrating to watch people be unhappy, especially if we feel that there are concrete steps they could take that would improve their circumstances. Sometimes, our challenge is to insulate and protect ourselves from the depressing cloud they spread, rather than to think that we can help them.

You can certainly spread your own smile around or even deliver an occasional flower, humorous or inspirational book, or some other token that says, "I'm thinking of you." If she is receptive to talk of faith, you can follow that pathway. You can certainly pray for her. But there is nothing you can do that can take control of this woman's life and force her to live it in another way.

Rabbi Daniel and Susan Lapin

98.
Gender Neutral Language

My church is divided over whether to use 'Chairman' (for both genders), or the more generic and PC version of 'Chair' or 'Chairperson' as the title for the head of a committee.

How do we resolve this issue?

Pari

Dear Pari,

What an interesting question. As writers, we constantly need to choose whether to repeatedly use the cumbersome language 'he or she' or, for example, to say mail carrier instead of assuming that people will recognize that mailman references a job, not a gender.

We can certainly find instances in the Bible where the word 'man' is meant to specify masculine human beings as well as other instances where it includes all humanity. When the verse specifies woman, on the other hand, it is limiting the meaning to females only. We can only think that for centuries our language copied this precedence so that man could mean masculine human beings or it could mean mankind in the broader sense.

However, gender neutrality and its partner gender specificity are certainly part of today's daily culture. There are instances where the change in language makes sense and others where it is an offering to the god of political correctness. Rather than weighing in on your congregation's dilemma, we'd like to suggest that your committee asks itself why this is a big issue. Could the language debate be revealing a tendency to bicker over petty matters or perhaps a substantial dissatisfaction among the women involved? It would seem to me that adults could opt to let whomever the chair(man) is choose how (he or she) wants to be addressed or allow each person to use whatever title comes naturally to (his or her) tongue.

If this issue is truly divisive and people are spending time on it rather than doing productive work or going home to their families, then it seems to us that a re-evaluation of more than language is needed.

Rabbi Daniel and Susan Lapin

99.
Does Everything Happen
for a Reason?

Is it Biblical to believe that "Everything happens for a reason?"

Evelyn

Dear Evelyn,

Yes and no. (You didn't expect a straightforward answer, did you?)

By yes, we mean that a Biblical worldview mandates that life is not random and accidental. Our lives and the lives of those who came before us and who will follow us are in some ways playing out a grand design that only God knows and understands.

However, we must also avoid the trap of relinquishing responsibility for our lives and living like a victim of circumstance. It would be completely wrong, for example, to take drugs, commit a crime, lose my family and job and then console myself by saying that all these bad things are happening as some part of God's grand design. No, these things are happening because God gives us free choice and I decided to mess up my life. In this sense, we have to answer your question with a 'no.'

While God oversees each of our lives, there are times that all of us are caught up in the larger picture. If someone loses a job in a time of prosperity a different type of introspection is needed than right now when one may simply be caught up as part of a company's massive layoffs.

While we do believe that there is a reason for each thing that happens, we would still focus on trying to extract a message for growth from all of life's happenings. That could mean accepting personal responsibility when appropriate and sometimes it means forging courageously ahead even though we don't understand everything that is happening to us.

Rabbi Daniel and Susan Lapin

100.
My Friends Seem Irritated
by My Christianity

I am a Christian with a deep Jewish heritage and while I am firm in my Christian faith, feel a deep connection with the Jewish people. I love and defend the Jews (and Israel!) completely.

How do I marry the two parts of myself which are not, in reality, mutually exclusive? Too often, I find my Jewish friends skeptical or somewhat irritated by Christianity.

Sarah B.

Sarah,

Quite frankly, it sounds like you have very smoothly integrated your Christian faith with your connection with the Jewish people. The real question doesn't seem to be yours, but instead why your friends have a problem.

Not knowing you or your friends, we can't be sure we are on the right track, but here are a few points to ponder and perhaps actions to take:

1)   How knowledgeable are your friends about either Judaism or Christianity? The less the current generation of Jews knows about either, the more skeptical and irritated they are in general. Sadly, Jews ignorant of the beliefs and practices of the Torah tend to view their Jewish identity exclusively in

terms of not believing in Jesus. That makes them antagonistic to Christianity.

2)   We would advise giving as a present a book like Corrie ten Boom's *The Hiding Place* to your friends. This book and others like it are incredibly eye opening to Jews who mistakenly associate Nazism with Christianity (as presented by media and academia) and furthermore assume that any friendship to Jews from Christians is based on the desire to proselytize.

3)   Don't be defensive. While we suggest focusing on the friendship and avoiding confrontation, you certainly shouldn't have to hide your Christianity or your appreciation of Judaism. If appropriate, turn the tables. Use phrases like, "I am hearing that you don't respect my religion, and I find that offensive. I believe we are all entitled to our beliefs."

Wishing you well,

Rabbi Daniel and Susan Lapin

101.
Crossing Privacy and Intimacy Barriers With Others in Our Lives

What was the Hebrew word you used about a month ago that had two meanings? It meant closeness or intimacy and it also meant being associated with. Will you explain this again?

Cheryl B.

Dear Cheryl,

You are referring to an episode we filmed for our *Ancient Jewish Wisdom Show* on TCT. We looked at Numbers 22, the story of Balaam, and showed how it made no sense in the English translation. It looks like God tells Balaam to go with the officers of Moab and then gets angry with him for going with them. The Hebrew, on the other hand, uses two different words for with—'et' and 'im'. Once you know the Hebrew, God's instructions and response to Balaam make complete sense.

Scripture becomes clear in other places as well when you know the secret of these two Hebrew words. As we said on the show, when we fly in a commercial airliner we are "with" hundreds of other people. That is entirely different from the way we might go for a walk "with" a friend.

The take-away value is that we want to make sure that we are interacting closely with those to whom we wish to be close, while not crossing privacy and intimacy barriers with others in our lives. Protecting ourselves by dividing people into different categories of this type is a reality for all of us who function in school, in the workplace, in our communities and in the larger world.

Thank you for giving us the opportunity to review this material,

Rabbi Daniel and Susan Lapin

Enjoy These Additional Books & Audio CDs
from Lifecodex Publishing

Available at www.RabbiDanielLapin.com

Enjoy These Additional Books & Audio CDs
from Lifecodex Publishing

Biblical Blueprint Audio Set

Audio
CD

Includes: Let My People Go
The 10 Commandments • Perils of Profanity
Day for Atonement • Festival of Lights

DVD's and Special Edition Books

DVD

Paperback

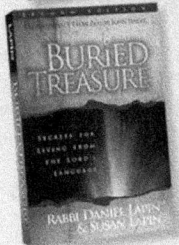

Hardcover

Includes:
Ancient Jewish Wisdom vol. 1
Ancient Jewish Wisdom vol. 2
Thought Tools Book vol. 1
Thought Tools Book vol. 2
Buried Treasure Book

Available at www.RabbiDanielLapin.com

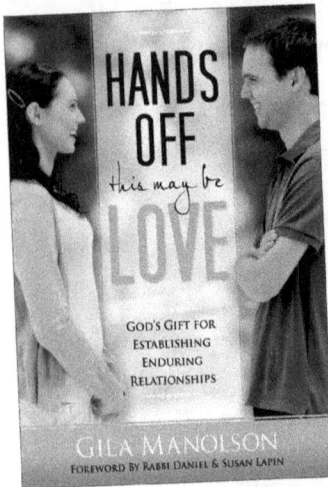

Hands Off!
This May Be Love

God's Gift for Establishing
Enduring Relationships

by
Gila Manolson

Available now at
www.RabbiDanielLapin.com

Gila Manolson's book, *Hand's Off! This May Be Love*, is one of the best and most needed books we've read in a long time... She eloquently describes the importance of not only honoring and respecting the opposite sex but also honoring and respecting yourself enough to wait before you build those powerful connections brought through touch...

Thanks for a marvelous read!

Pastors Mark and Vicki Biltz
Church for All Nations, Tacoma, WA

Filled with ancient wisdom and modern humor, this groundbreaking book provides insights into succeeding at love that have never been heard. While some will reject the author's premise outright, many others will take her sound advice to heart. Those who are smart enough to do so will surely reap many rewards. For this book, young people and their parents owe the author an enormous debt.

Miriam Grossman, MD
Author of Unprotected and You're Teaching My Child WHAT!

This book is important, bold, and to some, even controversial. The principles presented are sound and hold the potential to turn the cultural tide. They address one of the greatest needs in our time and present a worthy challenge to the current generation. The future is literally in the balance teetering between moral depravity and purity. Read this book and share it with someone who needs to hear its truth.

Pastors Mike and Kathy Hayes
Covenant Church, Dallas, TX

www.ingramcontent.com/pod-product-compliance
Lightning Source LLC
LaVergne TN
LVHW091215080426
835509LV00009B/999